"This is the best book of its [...] of paragraphs I want to captu[...] with each chapter. I want all my clients, family members, and friends to have a copy. Terri Dean has such an insightful way of expressing the 'growth and wholeness moments' that bridge to the deeply human sacredness we all share. Terri Clements Dean is a gifted writer and psychotherapist. I hope she keeps writing!"

— Mary Ellen Hughes, LCSW, psychotherapist

"This book is inspirational at a deep level of the psyche. Dr. Terri Dean is masterful in teaching us about wholeness in a delightful, down-to-earth manner. Her writings resonated with me personally in some areas of my own life. The book should be helpful to anyone who is a seeker."

— Harold W. Haddle Jr., PhD, psychologist, writer, and author of *Seeking Is Finding*

"Not enough words, how wonderful this book! The stories in *Grace Notes* are sacred, powerful, inspiring, and moving. It made me think in a deep way about the themes of redemption, love, and grace, making way for wholeness. It is one of the most beautiful books I've had the privilege to read."

— Joan Daniel, addictions counselor

"With humor, compassion, and a heartfelt desire to support others, Terri Clements Dean embarks with each of us on a journey toward wholeness. Her words are generous gems of wisdom to carry along the way."

— Beth McKibben-Nee, MLIS

"Dr. Dean's personal stories and stories about her clients are a perfect blend of holiness and practicality. It is evident that the book is a labor of love. *Grace Notes* flow freely throughout the book, engaging the reader in the moment. Everything from the title to the quotes, from the content to the appendixes, is beautifully done. *Grace Notes* is every bit as inspirational as anything published by well-known authors like Wayne Dyer, Joel Osteen, Richard Rohr, and C. S. Lewis. In my opinion, this book deserves to be on the bestseller list."

— Linda Lanzarotta, banker

"Dr. Dean has written a fabulous *theory of relativity* for humans. A rare experience of thought, personal history, and useful conclusions. An important piece in the puzzle of life. Enjoy!"

— R. Thomas Hughes, entrepreneur

"This is quite simply a beautiful book. With courage and compassion, the author reminds us that we are all on a journey to wholeness and never without hope. An important read for anyone who sometimes struggles to make sense of it all."

— Dianne, educator

"What I like most is that the author gives us stories rather than telling us what to do to make our lives better. I read one or two at a time and let them sink in before moving on and, with my busy schedule, that was helpful. I hope she writes more."

— Brian, attorney and financial advisor

OTHER BOOKS BY TERRI CLEMENTS DEAN

Traveling Stories: Lessons from the Journey of Life

*Traveling Stories Journal: A Guide to Discovering
Your Own Life Lessons*

GRACE
NOTES

TRAVELING THE PATH OF WHOLENESS

Terri Clements Dean

TERRI CLEMENTS DEAN, PhD

LIFESTORY PUBLISHING
ORLANDO, FLORIDA

Grace Notes:
Traveling the Path of Wholeness

LifeStory Publishing
P. O. Box 541527
Orlando, FL 32854

ISBN-10: 1-939472-26-1
ISBN-13: 978-1-939472-26-7

Library of Congress Control Number: 2017946583

Printed in the United States of America

Cover and interior design by Joan Keyes,
    Dovetail Publishing Services & Legacies
Cover photo by Carol K. Walsh
Author photo by Kellie Boston, Boston Photography

First Edition: July 2017
10 9 8 7 6 5 4 3 2

DEDICATION

For my mothers and fathers, by birth and by grace,
and, always—for Mark

GRACE NOTES

The handwritten notes that open each section are excerpts from the journals I've kept off and on since I was old enough to write. Sometime in the early 1980s, I began paying attention to the moments of unexpected joy or unlikely solutions that showed up in my life, and some days I remembered to write them down. They became my grace notes and ultimately the title for this book. These notes remind me that wherever I find myself on my path of wholeness, I am never entirely on my own; that, if I keep trudging forward to the best of my ability, I will be given the help I need to make the journey.

NOTE TO READERS

I am a storyteller. I do not enjoy academic writing, although I'm endlessly grateful to those who do it. They contribute so much to our knowledge and understanding, and I've done just enough of it to know how diligent and precise they have to be to do it well.

But I love telling stories and I have this bizarre, perhaps totally insane, idea that when we really love doing a thing that is in its nature good, it carries its own moral imperative, that we indeed should do that. So I tell stories and hope that someone benefits at least a tiny bit as much as I do.

The stories I've offered here have come to me from many sources. Some came from clients or friends, some from my travels or my life, and some presumably out of thin air. One came from a bookmark that sat on my desk for three years before the morning I saw it for the zillionth time and said, oh, yes, I need to write that story.

The stories that include clients are entirely true even though many of the specific details have been changed to guard the privacy of the person. I'm not all that impressed with those "facts" in the first place, since they tend to change over time with memory and with new information, and because they are the least important part of any story. The most important part of any story is always how it illuminates the human condition or shared experience, and so in that way all these stories are true.

My personal stories are true enough in their way as well. I tell them as I remember them now: with full knowledge that memory is always sketchy and subject to constant revision as we grow and change and produce new stories. Still, these things happened and I've reported them as best I can with my current understandings.

Some of the stories here are not actual stories as such but could more rightly be called essays. I think of them as stories because everything I know and believe and hold dear was given me through the stories I've heard and seen and been part of making.

I know that I don't have the answers for anyone at all, sometimes not even myself, and neither I nor anyone else can or should tell another person how to grow up. I do have suggestions for what might be helpful based on what has been helpful for me and for others I've known. Some of these suggestions have good bases in research and some do not. Where they don't, it's primarily because they haven't been researched at all, being too fuzzy or too hard to reduce to testable hypotheses and replicable procedures. Like all systems of knowledge, science has its limits.

When they don't, please trust that I sincerely believe them to be helpful and also understand that they may not be helpful for everyone. We each have our own distinct path and yet we are all traveling together. Our stories connect us.

About quotes: About thirty years ago, I began saving quotes from articles or books I read that spoke to me in some way. Some of these were written in journals and some were tucked into a file or notebook. When I got my first computer and learned to use word processing programs, I began gradually accumulating all those bits and bobs into one file. They now number in the hundreds. I've tried wherever possible to verify the attributions. Some of them are easy to find on the Internet and others don't seem to be there anywhere, so I've gone back to original references and double-checked myself. Each one used in this book was chosen with care and offered in gratitude.

CONTENTS

PROLOGUE

Today –
    I'm grateful for:

My beautiful daughters,
Sunshine,
Flowers,
A red bird,
My car radio,
My cozy office,
Mark, of course,
Memories,
Freshly laundered Sheets

Journal Entry, 1995

Florida, 2009

THE PATH

A child is born. And thus begins the journey of wholeness. A young woman weeps and wonders when she will ever be happy. A father mourns the loss of his child. Another man rages against the injustice of life. A woman celebrates her success. Another woman is stunned by the doctor's words. An old man sits by the fire and reflects on the path he's traveled. And thus continues the journey of wholeness.

From the first breath to the last, we are all of us all of the time on the journey of wholeness. At times, the way is clear and the path even. Other times, many times, the path grows tangled or torn, strewn with debris and slippery from rain. No matter; the way forward is always forward, so on we go. We learn; we suffer; we endure; we adapt; we succeed—only to fall again. And we go on. Our destination is never known, only dreamed, and still we go on. We know with our heart's knowing that life is dear and limited and we must journey on, but we do not know why or how. Still, we go on.

Learning and unlearning mark the earliest years. What seemed true and inevitable at two no longer serves at five or seven. What worked at twenty is destructive at thirty. The best lessons become resources: the worst become wounds. And still we go on. We live and we grow and we become. Our talents emerge to welcome or

9

rejection, and we accommodate. Our interests meet opportunity or denial, and we grow or hide. We are loved and punished and accepted and rejected and neglected and nurtured and injured, and we become in response to them all.

We learn to love and to explore and to create and to worship. We also learn to hide and deceive and repress and destroy. No life is without suffering; none without joy. We are prone to both sin and service. Some of our actions cause harm, but we also do good. The path is uneven; the way often unclear. And still we go on.

We may begin to seek answers or solutions within and without. Confusion fires the quest for greater clarity. We need answers to the big questions—questions of identity, belonging, and meaning—and directions for the path. Depending on our individual natures, we may try to figure it all out on our own, or we may go searching for help. Some of us, perhaps most of us, do both.

That quest may lead us to right answers or wrong, and still we go on. We try again and again and again. We read books, follow gurus, go on diets, go to therapy, read more books, ask our friends, and watch our neighbors. We seek out practical solutions and spiritual guidance. We grow and we learn. We succeed and we fail. We celebrate and we suffer. We fall short of perfection and wonder how to live with that. Or we lose hope and retreat into depression or anger. And still we go on.

What we weren't told and didn't know is that life is a journey toward wholeness and that wholeness isn't identical to happiness or success or self-actualization or anything that even resembles perfection. Wholeness is instead the sum of ourselves—the pain, the insecurities, the failings and failures, in combination with our gifts, our instincts, our finest qualities, and our hopes and our dreams. Wholeness is all of who we are, our undiminished entirety—seen, accepted, treasured, redeemed, and restored to rightful possession. We simply must get to know ourselves, accept ourselves, and work hard to become the best of that, while continuing the walk with all of its inherent hills and valleys.

To do that, to make the journey, we will need to equip ourselves with certain essentials—honesty, compassion, patience, forgiveness, fortitude, curiosity, and love. When these are lost, as they will be, we must find them again. We will need help. We will need faith that help will come when we can't see it coming or imagine its arrival. We will need other people. We will choose them wisely or wrongly, and then we will choose again. The blessing is that the path is long and, in its way, forgiving. Mistakes will be made—they are there for the learning.

The newborn and the old man are walking the path. Both are whole and wholly themselves and yet, in some way, not yet known and accepted. That is the mystery. Life itself is our best teacher, and she carries us forward in knowledge and in mystery for reasons we may never understand. But isn't that the way of paths anyhow? You can only see where you are and where you've just been, with a bit of what lies ahead. The parts you've already traveled become memory, only partially recalled, and the path ahead lies in darkness. Still, you go on. And as you walk, the path becomes the place you inhabit, your home, your life, and your future. You have only to walk with awareness, with love, and with the sure and certain knowledge that grace will clear the way.

The most terrifying thing is to accept oneself completely.

—Carl Jung, Swiss psychiatrist and founder of depth analysis

PART I

I was working in the yard &
decided some hanging pots out
in the garden needed water. I
got the hose & stood on the patio
and sprayed them for a while—
me about 20 feet away—and
a male cardinal came to take
a shower! He flew right into
the pot I was watering and
stayed a long time with all sorts
of wing flapping and feather
ruffling. He was clearly loving
his bath and I so loved giving
it to him. Joy!

Journal Entry, 1999

St. John's River, 2015

Florida, 2001

WHOLENESS

Wholeness: the state of being free of injury; having all its proper parts or components; constituting the total sum or undiminished entirety; constituting an undivided unit.

—*Merriam-Webster Dictionary*

Once upon a time, I believed there was a secret to happiness, a secret others knew and, for some reason, wouldn't share with me. I thought the fault was mine somehow, though I couldn't understand when or how I had gone wrong. I spent a great deal of time and energy trying to figure it all out. Perhaps it was because I wasn't pretty enough or smart enough or, with attitudes partially shaped by growing up in the American South in the second half of the twentieth century, maybe I had sinned and fallen from grace.

So I tried harder. I got a nose job, lost weight, changed jobs or husbands, and attended churches and synagogues and new age conclaves. I went back to school and got more education and then more again. I went to therapy, once, twice, three times, and I remained unhappy. I coped, as people do, in a variety of ways, some helpful and healthful, some profoundly destructive, but I coped and I kept looking for the answers, the secret that would open the door to happiness. I thought, if only I can correct this one other thing about myself, then I will be happy because then I will be perfect.

How was I to know that the fundamental flaw was not in me, but in the journey I had chosen? Seeking perfection, I blinded myself to the possibility of wholeness. I wanted to be something I was not, rather than all of who I am and may be. I wanted to be different when I only needed to be more of myself.

Perfection is a cold, hard, narrow kind of a thing. Paradoxically, it is also either a given or an impossible achievement. Either everything is perfect exactly as it is, or perfection is unattainable because change is constant. If happiness is based on finding perfection, then there is little chance of happiness.

Wholeness is softer, warmer, and much, much wider. Wholeness has room for change, as well as complexity, error, difference, and learning, for comedy and tragedy, for curiosity and imagination, for humor, laughter, love, and disappointment. Wholeness is not a destination nor is it something we attain or achieve, but rather something we experience and then forget but never lose. We can't hold onto it, but we can live within its flow, and within our wholeness, happiness and joy emerge, impermanent and fluid, but also radiant and reliable.

Having failed spectacularly in my quest for perfection, I was forced to notice the path of wholeness. Happiness, or something like it, was waiting there. Being permanently human, I continue to find obstacles along the way, within and without. I wonder and wander and occasionally go off course, but the path is kind and patient and allows my return. I am grateful.

The self is a calm stable center surrounded by a continuous changing sea. Merge with yourself and be ready for any emergent sea.

—Coretta Scott King, American civil rights leader

1

PSYCHOTHERAPY 1
THE DOCTOR

Our deepest calling is to grow into our own authentic self-hood,
whether or not it conforms to some image of who we ought to be.
As we do so, we will not only find the joy that every human being
seeks—we will also find our path of authentic service in the world.

— Parker Palmer, American author and educator

I made my first visit to a psychotherapist when I was twenty-five. This particular therapist was a male psychiatrist back in the days when those folks still did talk therapy. Dr. Nolan's office was dark, the only light coming from a desk lamp and a single floor lamp in a corner; it was furnished with leather, and I recall a small footstool that he rested his feet on, one crossed over the other at the ankle. There were books and files and soft music playing. He smoked a pipe, and there was a mug of coffee or tea on the table by his chair. Perhaps he stood to welcome me or perhaps not, but he waved me to the chair opposite his and said, "Why have you come today?" and I said, "I'm not happy and I should be." Everything he needed to know about me was contained in that sentence, although I can't say if he was wise enough then to know. I certainly wasn't.

I don't recall the details of that session or any of the others we had. The memories I have are small flashes of moments, a comment from him, something I said, a feeling, or an image. I know we ended the therapy when Dr. Nolan told me he thought he couldn't treat me anymore because, "I like you too much." It tells you a lot about me at that time that I didn't ask what he meant by that or why that would mean we needed to stop. I didn't know the answer to either of those questions, but I was too proud to admit it—I thought I should know—and also too fearful that whatever answer he gave might hurt me somehow. So we stopped. Here's what I learned from that therapy experience:

- I was probably depressed and certainly anxious.
- Perhaps other people and life circumstances were part of the problems I blamed myself for.
- My history had contributed to the ways I handled things now.
- I could say a few things out loud I had never spoken before, but only a few.
- And for some reason I still can't explain, talking with someone about these things, even ever so cautiously, seemed to help.

I stole those therapy hours. My husband, James, liked to maintain strict control of everything in his life, including me and our money. I had told him I wanted to see someone because I was unhappy. I asked him to go with me, but he said no, it was a waste of time and I should be able to work out my own problems. He certainly had no need to talk with some overeducated phony, and he refused to allow me to go either. We had good insurance, which would have covered this treatment, but I couldn't file it since James would surely have discovered evidence of my visits, so I saved money from my allowances for lunch and for groceries and made the appointments during my lunch hour at work. Oh, yes, I had a good job and made decent wages, which I turned over to James or at least deposited into our joint account from which I paid the bills, but which he monitored closely. I doubt I told the psychiatrist any of this. It seemed normal to me. I did know I was a thief because I took the money to pay for my therapy dishonestly. I also knew that somehow I had to save my own life, and this was the only thing I could think to do.

Therapy didn't entirely cure my presenting problem: that I was unhappy and felt I shouldn't be. I left there just as unhappy, but slightly less sure that I shouldn't be. Something in those hours suggested to me that perhaps, just perhaps, my perceptions of my life were valid, and maybe at least some of the problems were in my life rather than in me. I began with the firm conviction that there was something deeply wrong with me that needed fixing in order for me to be happy. True enough in its way, but it didn't also mean I had to accept *everything* and find a way to be happy. Maybe it would be all right to ask for a few things for myself or to say no to a few things other people wanted me to tolerate.

When I made my first appointment, I didn't know what to expect, and most of my visits left me more confused than anything else, but I continued to go because, surprisingly, Dr. Nolan seemed to listen to me, to like me, and to agree with some of my thinking. That therapist loved me a little, and a little bit of me was healed. Something was redeemed. I received grace. I didn't know it then, but these would become the themes of my life—grace, love, and redemption. I think they are the themes of all our lives.

I do not at all understand the mystery of grace—only that it meets us where we are but does not leave us where it found us.

—Anne Lamott, American author

2

REDEEMING THE SELF

Character—the willingness to accept responsibility for one's
own life—is the source from which self-respect springs.
—Joan Didion, American novelist and journalist

Not so many years after my sessions with Dr. Nolan, I was working as a clinical psychologist in private practice. One morning, one of my clients, Dina, said as she was leaving my office at the end of her last appointment, "Well, I'm just going out there now and live me!" I can't imagine a more positive outcome for a therapy experience than that—to be able to go forward living as oneself. I knew she would do it, too, because I had been the grateful and gratified witness to her journey of reclaiming herself.

There is no abandonment so devastating nor any so common as the abandonment of self. When we move away from our true selves into attempts to become someone different, or lose touch with our feelings and instincts, we enter a world of fear and loneliness, and yet that is what most of us do to some extent or other. The necessary adjustments for participation in families and in the larger social context inevitably result in some loss of self. Mother is impatient with the child's boisterousness. Father requires a manly son. At school, teachers say sit still and be quiet. The other kids make fun of a girl's hairstyle. A boy is the last one chosen for basketball because of his clumsiness. And he thinks, *I must change this*. Or he doesn't think at all, but silently, gradually, tries to make himself into someone who fits better, someone who is praised and not criticized, someone who pleases.

And it works pretty well, so he doubles his efforts and tries it again when new expectations come along.

Maybe along the way, a young girl learns that this feeling or that one isn't pleasing to others or puts her or someone else at perceived risk, so she learns to push those feelings aside, to suppress them if she can or remain silent if she can't eliminate them altogether. She even learns that she shouldn't feel that way, that her feelings aren't valid, and she accepts that and begins to judge them negatively herself. She thinks, *I shouldn't feel so angry (sad, lonely, envious, eager, discouraged, happy): there must be something wrong with me.* She denies the feelings more strongly, and they go underground and emerge only in excess or in symptom.

My childhood, like that of many others, was a happy/sad/scary/ lonely/cherished kind of a thing. It was very confusing. Most of the time, I didn't know what I felt, but I did know that certain displays of emotion caused problems. My parents sincerely wanted me to be happy for all the right reasons, but also because my sadness on top of theirs would be too much to handle. So I learned to show happiness and repress the rest. I learned the lesson well and was largely effective. Not long before my father died at the age of eighty-nine, I heard him tell a gathering, "Terri was always a happy child." I wondered whom he was talking about. What I best recalled was how frightened and sad I was much of the time. I am sure he had no idea. That's partially because he was so good at staying away through busyness and his own particular brand of emotional distance, but it's also because I was damned good at looking happy. I kept the other things to myself. Indeed, I did such a good job, I was scarcely aware of them myself.

That continued well into adulthood. I never told a soul about the abuse and unkindness that marked my first marriage. People, even the closest ones, were shocked when they learned I was divorcing my husband. Why wouldn't they be? I looked happy enough. I had copied my father and used busyness and earnest endeavor as my sedatives. I didn't let myself feel. It took years for me to admit to myself just how miserable I was and even longer to decide to trust that feeling and let it carry me forward. In fact, I'm not sure I did learn to trust it. I just knew I would die if I stayed, and I wanted to live.

There was one funny thing, though, throughout this time. If I happened to see a sad movie or read a sad story, I would cry, not a few gentle tears, but sobs so hard and so strong that they embarrassed or disturbed anyone nearby. I couldn't control it. I found it baffling, too, since I prided myself on my emotional control. I didn't know then that emotions can't be eradicated—they can only be postponed or diverted.

Then came the day when all that I had buried came bursting through in the form of what, looking back, I can see as an emotional collapse and explosion. My own personal earthquake, when the ground split open and all the structures came tumbling down, leaving my external and internal life in rubble. This bit of self-assurance lying upside down on the wrong side of the road, that bit of confidence burnt to a cinder, that shell of hard-earned competence useless in the new environment.

And that was a blessing. Left with nothing to rely on, I could start again and rebuild from the ground up. The surprise came when I realized that my own instincts, my own emotions, would need to be the foundation, that without them I was without substance and would collapse again. I had to learn to listen to the voice within, even when it seemed like bad news, and be willing to hear its message. I had to accept that all of my feelings had a place and deserved my respect. I had to try to trust that my desires and interests mattered and could be attended to without harming others. I had to discover who I was from the inside out, rather than from the outside in.

And if I did, when I did, I would have something to offer. It would be enough. It would be good. Because only when I could know myself could I be accountable for myself and to myself. I don't know when it happened or just how, nor do I know who is to blame, if anyone is, but I do know that I abandoned myself early on, and only when I could reclaim myself could I truly accept responsibility for my actions, my thoughts, my feelings, my choices. When I failed to do that, I was left with the doomed option of assigning those responsibilities to someone else, for whom it could only be an impossible task. They failed and I hated them for it, and in the deepest recesses of my spirit and soul, I hated myself for abdicating.

It all begins with me. No matter the whys and wherefores of my self-abandonment, no matter the excellence of the cause I was serving in denying myself; until I allow myself to be known in all my messy glory, I am stuck wherever I am. I can only repeat the patterns and receive the outcomes they produce. I don't have choices, only reactions. So whether I like what I see at first or not, little matter; I must face my truth and choose myself. Oh, so I really am selfish and petty. Okay. I choose me. Oh, so I really am scared and tentative and shy. Okay. I choose me. Oh, so I really am a terrible cook. Okay. I choose me. Oh, so I am energetic and kind and compassionate and eager and curious. Okay. I choose me.

When I look back through my life and see the mistakes I've made, the cruelties I've enacted, my negligence, my pride, my insensitivity, I feel shame. Okay, I choose me, and I choose to feel that shame and let it guide me, not own me. When I try to pretend I didn't do those things or act that way or try to blame someone else for the things I've done, I am stuck wherever I am. When I run from that shame, I must ever keep on running, because the shame has nowhere to go and nothing to do but shadow me. It is, after all, mine.

But if I stop running and let it catch up to me, meet it head-on and hear what it's trying to say, I can learn and I can heal and I can redeem the shame and allow it to become what it can. I've seen shame turn into compassion and humility, into love and even laughter. I've seen it lead a person from the depths of despair to the heights of joy. And the same is true for any denied feeling or repressed regret. Unwelcomed, they pursue, and in fleeing, we run away from what's deepest and truest and best within us.

So it begins. I stop. I listen. I look. I say, yes, this is true. This is who I am and have been. If this is a mess, well, it's my mess. I will stand here and start here and begin with this and see where that takes me. I will learn what needs learning and do the work that needs doing, and I will grow and be taught and try and fail and sometimes succeed, but I will do it as myself and for myself and with myself. I will hold myself accountable, but I will also be kind to myself. I will stand with this me, the one with the scars and the secrets, the stories and alibis, the uncertainties and vanities. This me. Right now.

He who knows others is wise; he who knows himself is enlightened.

—Lao Tzu, ancient Chinese philosopher and founder of Taoism

3

PAY ATTENTION

*Attention, taken to its highest degree, is the same thing as prayer.
It presupposes faith and love.*

—Simone Weil, French philosopher and author

L
ife itself is our best teacher. She offers all the lessons we will
ever need abundantly and without restraint. If we miss them
the first time, they will be offered again and again until we are
ready to learn.

Our part—the work of wholeness—is to be honest with ourselves
and others, to pay careful attention to the messages we receive, to
trust the process, and to be diligent in applying what we learn to our
lives.

For most of us, the honesty part is the first hurdle. It's so much
more comfortable to ignore or deny the ways we let ourselves down.
Our defenses are there for a reason. They protect us from knowing
those truths we were in fact unable to bear at a certain time in our
lives. We create stories in our heads to help us endure until the time
is right for the truth to emerge. We also deny and ignore aspects of
ourselves that seemed unwelcome to important people in our early
lives. This is how we survive. We build a self and a worldview that
allows us to function adequately where we are.

But there comes a time when the defenses no longer work and
when the story we've created is too small, too restrictive, to carry us
forward. We begin to see what we could not see before, and we find
we can no longer bear the burden of dishonesty. The walls start to

crumble, and we begin to see truths that were hidden before. This can be terrifying or liberating—or both at the same time. Still, we are called to shed the protective skin, and there comes a time when we have no choice. Certain true things refuse to be denied any longer, and we find that honesty is in fact the first step toward living the lives we were meant to live.

On this platform of honesty, we can begin to build our awareness and to pay attention to the messages and signs that come our way. The tiniest step toward greater authenticity frees hidden reserves of power and potential. If we aren't busy trying to *not* know something, we have more energy to recognize precisely the messages life is sending to us. It takes enormous energy to maintain even the smallest deception. We must daily make the commitment to be as honest with ourselves as we possibly can and to extend that same honesty outward to others. Courage is called for.

Once we begin to live a life based on honesty, we start to pay attention to what has passed us by before. We become alert to behaviors, patterns, yearnings, and intuitions we may have missed in the past. We can teach ourselves to attend to our inner selves, to our deepest longings, and to our greatest fears. These are teachers, and their lessons are essential. Thoughts, feelings, daydreams, night dreams, symptoms, symbols, and synergies begin to emerge as meaningful and beneficent. They bring unexpected gifts of expansion or coherence to our lives.

This paying attention is much broader and richer than one first imagines. It barely resembles what is so often referred to in popular culture as mindfulness, a general term often used to refer to meditative practices, though its fuller meaning implies a broader focus on the present moment. While there is no doubt that meditation has an important part to play in spiritual practice as well as healthful living and that learning to center oneself in the moment is an important correction to the sensory bombardment and multitasking of the current era, the sort of attention that is required for wholeness is not limited to specific periods set aside each day or to specific activities nor even to the present moment.

This attention must be carried about all day long and applied to one's inner life as well as the outer world. You really have to notice how you feel, what your intuition tells you, where your dreams are pointing, and the symptoms that show where your injuries lie. You have to watch your behavior. And you have to ask questions about it all. How does one thing match up with the other? What might this symptom mean? Why this feeling now? Mind, senses, intuition, and understanding join and work together to make sense of experience.

And this hard work is not limited to your inner life. It is also necessary to pay attention to the world around you and notice, really notice, what passes your way. Are there patterns in how people respond to you? What messages are being sent your way? How do other people live? How are their choices different from yours? Who can you learn from? What do you see/hear/smell/taste/feel in the course of a day? Have you noticed any symbols or themes recurring around you? Is there a lesson there somewhere?

And of course, you must also go on living your life in this very moment, doing your best and hoping for better tomorrow. You must carry on loving and working and praying and planning. The pathway to wholeness, it turns out, doesn't lead to the mountaintop, but right to your front door. It's found where you are—within your whole-hearted involvement with the life you have now and the one you are creating day by day.

Grace is the courage to be at home in the moving resonance of the present.

—Sam Keen, American author and philosopher

4

AWAKENING

Your vision will become clear only when you can look into your own heart. Who looks outside, dreams; who looks inside, awakes.

—Carl Jung, Swiss psychiatrist and founder of analytic psychology

Most of the time when people make their first appointment with me, they are in search of answers. They hope I will be able to show them a way out of whatever muddle they find themselves in, that I will have a (hopefully) quick solution to their dilemma, some words I will say or advice I can give to start them down the right path.

That was true for me as well. When I entered therapy, I was motivated by the need for answers and the hope the therapist had them. Surely someone trained in the complexities of human nature would know more than me and be able to give clear and precise directions for what I should do to make my life better, to cure my unhappiness.

Every beginning psychotherapy relationship must in due time come to terms with the clients' disappointment when they learn this is not true. None of my therapists had the answers for me, nor do I have them for my clients. Oh, I have answers galore, but I'm never sure which would be the correct one for any particular client until the client teaches me by discovering his or her own.

What I can do, and what every good therapy does, is help the client wake up. In order to grow as human beings, we must shed the illusions and delusions that keep us asleep and stuck in the shadows of the past or the lies of the present. It is not possible to become the person we need to become when we are trapped in the fictional world we created in order to endure or survive what came before. What keeps us comfortable can also enslave us.

And so it is that the early part of any good therapy is often frankly miserable. One must step out of one's comfort zone, question closely held ideas, and drop all pretense for therapy to work. Nothing will change while we sleep, but letting go of illusion can be frightening and disorienting. If I am not this, then who am I? If not this life, then what life?

Some folks don't stick. When they don't, I think that's right for them. It's not the time for it. I don't get to judge. I just get to help if I can. And that's plenty for me. But, oh, when they do, what a journey we make—the client as explorer of mystery and discoverer of truth, and me as the most privileged witness and companion.

The first step is the holy one. A single moment of letting go and moving out into unknowing creates a portal through which one may walk toward self-awareness. The process of coming to self is one of awakening, claiming, mourning, and celebrating. Each person's unique journey is a reflection of all other individual journeys, of the whole human story. We can know ourselves because others have gone before and have told their stories. We can become because others have done so.

And yet our own growing is always profoundly individual. My truth may not be your truth and yours likely isn't mine, but still we learn from each other, and we provide for each other the materials and ground for the growing. I am able to stand here at this place in my life and with this level of assurance because others have shared their struggles and triumphs with me and because others have walked with me through mine. *We* can mourn and learn and claim and celebrate—I alone cannot. I am too weak, too small, too afraid, and too inexperienced to create a good life on my own. But we can. You and

I. My first and last therapist and I. My friend Linda and I. My husband, Mark, and I. You and I. All of us together can do what I alone could not.

I wish you had my answers. I know you don't. I wish I could rest in my fairy tale world, but I can't. I wish I didn't have to work so hard at growing up, but I do. It's necessary if I want to thrive and to live a good life. And it's also necessary because I won't leave myself alone. There's a force, an energy, a power within me that pushes me onward, that won't let me settle, that demands that I continue to grow. Resistance is possible, but it inevitably leads to either disaster or disaffection. I know because I have allowed it and allow it still from time to time, but always the pain of doing so breaks the spell and pushes me back to awareness. I simply must wake up and take the next holy step into mystery and onward toward wholeness. The difference is that now I know I never walk alone and that love and grace accompany me, and I know as well that the price of unconsciousness is more than I'm willing to pay.

Every truth I've claimed has added to my life in previously unimagined ways, even the hardest ones. The darkest memories and most shameful secrets have, when brought up and out, lost their power to harm and have become the springboards to some unexpected resource or place of connection. Some things needed grieving and some things needed restitution and some things were exposed as lies or deceptions, but ultimately all of them took me to a place of greater peace, freedom, or compassion. No exceptions.

So it is with great good faith that I can encourage awakening in others because I have seen and felt the power of its emergence. I can trust my client will be helped by seeing himself or herself more clearly, and I can hold that faith firmly until it can be passed on. This is so because we are part of the human story, and the human story is many-hued and yet all of one piece, as mysteries often are. We walk the same ground and carry similar loads, and in the most fundamental of ways, we are all in this together. Your healing is my healing, and my success is also yours. We awaken together, and every first holy step is on behalf of us all.

Wholeness is never lost, only forgotten.

—Rachel Naomi Remen, American physician and author

5

PAST AND PRESENT

Genuine forgiveness does not deny anger but faces it head-on.

—Alice Miller, Swiss psychologist and author

Lisa was thirty and a new mother when her psychiatrist referred her to me for treatment of postpartum depression. He planned to follow her as well and would manage her medication, but he felt she also needed someone to talk with about her feelings and about the meaning of this new role. Lisa was happy to comply, she said, because she wanted more than anything to be a good mother, and she worried that her symptoms would interfere with her parenting.

Lisa began our first session by talking about her marriage, which she described as a dream come true, and her joy when she learned she was expecting her first child. She and her husband both enjoyed the pregnancy and were then shocked and appalled when the birth left Lisa listless, tearful, and frightened. Postpartum depression is very common and is usually totally unrelated to the mother's maternal feelings. It has more to do with hormones than emotion, but since the inner experience seems to be a feeling experience, it is disheartening and confusing to the woman who has it and to those around her. Education helps, and by the time Lisa made her way to me, she had learned a great deal about what she was going through and had relief from the worst of the symptoms. The word she used to describe her current feeling was "disappointment." "I thought these would be the happiest days of my life. I waited to have a child until I felt mature enough to handle it. I swore I would never be like my mother, and here I am—just like her. I am so worried about my child."

I asked in what way she was like her mother, and she told me the story of her childhood. Her parents divorced when she was an infant, and her father's role in her life gradually diminished over the next several years until, by the time she was seven, he no longer visited regularly and rarely contributed financially. She said that he had died from a drug overdose when she was nineteen, but "he was hard to miss, since I'd never seen him much anyway."

An only child and with few relatives nearby, she and her mother were close in their isolation. Left in the care of babysitters and day-care centers while Mom worked, Lisa developed excellent social skills, as well as competencies beyond her years. She helped with housework, laundry, and cooking, and became her mother's closest confidante. It was her job to soothe Mom's sadness and to fill her loneliness. Although the word "depression" wasn't used in the household, the adult Lisa described her mother as depressed and too needy to meet the needs of a growing child. Lisa was terrified that her child would suffer the same fate.

And then she said, "I don't want to blame my mother for anything. She worked hard all her life and still does, and she loves me and had to do it all by herself. It's not her fault."

Of course, Lisa was right. It's not her mother's fault. But if Lisa was to forgive herself, she would also need to forgive her mother, and despite what she thought at the time, she hadn't done that yet, and she hadn't done it because she had never allowed herself to get angry. It may be a paradox, but it's true nonetheless that unless we give full expression in some way to our anger, our forgiveness will never reach the places within us that need to be healed. It will be a forgiveness of the mind, not the heart; it will be a forgiveness of words, not the spirit. And without that heart/spirit forgiveness, we are bound to the past and to the roles that the past demanded.

One of the roles Lisa had to play to help her mother function was the role of counselor. She had to understand, to be compassionate, to comfort. Anger has no place in that role, and Lisa had never made room for anger in any area of her life, especially toward her mother. She couldn't. It just wasn't safe. But she could be, and was, furious with herself. Even knowing that her depression was the result of hormonal imbalances that were outside her control, she blamed herself for her lack of joy and punished herself with stories of how her child would be harmed.

I never assume that I know more about my clients than they know about themselves. I don't. I do know something about patterns and about processes, and I can sometimes notice when someone seems to be missing possible alternate interpretations of experience. I thought this might be true in Lisa's case, and I wondered out loud if she had ever been angry with her mother. She said of course she had, that sometimes in her teen years, she had acted out and stayed out too late or failed to do chores around the house. But again she assured me that this was just teenage rebellion and that she and her mother were very close and she would never do anything to hurt her mother. "But," she said, "I hope I can be a better mother to my child than she was to me."

This dance continued for a few sessions. I would suggest that some of the ways she talked about her mother suggested that she might still be a bit angry about something from the past. She would respond that no, she wasn't angry, she could certainly see how tough her mother had it and that she did the best she could. I would say, "Well, yes, of course, but what about her child?"

Smart, educated people like Lisa often have highly developed skill at avoiding unpleasant truth. She had spent a great deal of time and energy learning about human behavior and family dynamics. She wanted so badly to develop the knowledge to build a healthy family and to raise well-adjusted children. She could say calmly that she knew she didn't get that at home.

I kept wondering where the feeling was. She didn't sound angry or sad or ashamed or any of the things I'd come to expect when people talked about their childhood. She didn't even sound wistful or happy, just emotionally flat.

Our work together continued, and she brought in her daily struggles with holding her mood steady. We experimented with techniques to help with that, some of which helped and some didn't, but overall she was maintaining a healthy level, and she felt that she was moving in the right direction. Her psychiatrist was pleased with her progress, and he and I stayed in close touch.

Then one day Lisa came in and told me she had had an argument with her mother the day before. Mom, it seems, had told Lisa she needed to "Get your act together and leave off all these visits to doctors and therapists and just take care of your child." Lisa said, "How dare she? Who does she think she is? She didn't do such a great job of raising her child." She was furious. And then she started to cry and so began to heal. She told me later that she walked all the way through her rage and her pain in that one session. And that she was finally able to forgive her mother.

I think sometimes it does happen like that. Other times many sessions and much time are required to process and release and find the path to forgiveness. Of course, therapy is only one alternative for growth and healing. People manage without it all the time. But therapy is what I do, and it can serve as an exemplar of the processes that carry personal growth forward. In ordinary life, as in therapy, forgiveness can be gradual or sudden, but it always demands certain conditions. To forgive, we must honestly acknowledge our pain and our anger; we must allow ourselves to feel them, even if we disapprove of them, as we often do. Sharing with another person—whether therapist, friend, mentor, or spiritual advisor—helps to reduce the shame and unbind the confusions. When we've done as much of that as we need to do, and not before, a new sense will emerge of its own accord. It can't be forced by will or coercion. In the meantime, our job is to hold the energy, treat ourselves kindly, and avoid retaliation or blame. We must wait.

Lisa said that when she left my office that day, she felt free and sad and wanted most of all to talk with her mother and tell her all the feelings she had denied up to now. She wanted to tell her mother that she forgave her for failing her in the ways that she did. But she said she knew she couldn't do that, that her new awareness didn't mean that her mother was in the same place, nor did it entitle her to burden her mother with unanticipated painful confidences. She knew she should wait and hope for a time and place when she could talk with her mother about their shared history. She even hoped her mom would tell her more about that time from her point of view to help her understand. But for now, she must be the custodian of this changed attitude and find ways to express it without doing harm.

In the days and weeks that followed and as she continued her treatment and learned more and more about parenting, she began to relax and gain confidence in her ability to mother her daughter. She said to me one day, "I know I'll make mistakes with her, but she'll be all right, because I'm all right." And of course, she was. None of us makes it to adulthood unscarred. The people who rear us are human, and humans are prone to mistakes. It's only natural to feel pain when injured and anger when mistreated. So it seems that most of us bring some unresolved feelings into adulthood. Unacknowledged, unclaimed, they bind us to the past and haunt our present. Only forgiveness can release us, and only with that release are we free to grow into our best selves.

We don't forgive in order to condone or to excuse or even to heal that particular relationship, although that can be a benefit. We forgive so we can move on and so that, when we eventually, inevitably fail at something that matters, we will have a way of forgiving ourselves. What we can't forgive, we can't redeem, and it becomes our fate. Forgiveness opens the door to our destiny, our right and proper involvement with life.

Looking back over a lifetime it becomes clear that we must rest our case on the hope for grace rather than any claim of perfection. This much is certain: it is easier to get through a lifetime with an intact spirit by learning the art of repentance and forgiveness than by avoiding risks and mistakes.

—Sam Keen, American author and philosopher

6

WHAT WE SEE MATTERS

I think we are well advised to keep on nodding terms with the people we used to be, whether we find them attractive company or not.

—Joan Didion, American novelist and journalist

Not long ago, I found some photos of my family taken in the middle years of my first marriage. The photos were mistakenly placed in a storage box with photos of distant relatives of long ago, and I only found them because my daughter Julie got interested in genealogy and wondered if some of them might have names and dates that would help her research.

A few of the photos were taken when my first husband and I, with our two young children, made a trip to the beach for vacation. I was twenty-seven years old that year. At that time when I looked in the mirror, I saw a woman who was fat and ugly. When I looked at the photos from this distance in time, what I saw was a lovely young woman who was a nice, normal weight. I looked really good in that bathing suit!

If only I had known. If only I had been able to see myself more clearly then, how might my life have been different?

It is literally true that we see what we expect to see, and our expectations are shaped by our beliefs and our experience. I can't say today how I came to believe that I was ugly, but I know that I did believe that. My parents weren't cruel people, and I never heard that at home. In fact, they told me I was beautiful, but I remember clearly that I did not believe them. I thought they lied to make me feel better about myself or that they themselves were blinded by their love for me. How does a child decide something like that? I think perhaps the children I went to school with may have teased me in cruel ways because children do that, but I don't recall the incidents, so that's mere speculation.

I did have a period in early adolescence when I was fat. That is accurate, not a fault in perception. I have those photos, too. I know why I was fat then, and I know how that affected me. I knew it then. I was fat because I came home from school each day and ate Ritz crackers and peanut butter, or cookies if we had them, until I was stuffed, and then ate huge, Southern dinners with dessert. I ate because I was lonely and frightened and sad, and I didn't know anything else to do. I hated being fat and knew that it made me less attractive to my peers (boys and girls), but back then people didn't diet and I don't think I would have been able to follow one anyway. Food was what got me through.

I learned to see myself as fat, and maybe ugly just followed from that. I don't know. I do know that I was never a confident teenager and that many mistakes flowed from my self-doubt. I saw myself as flawed and deficient and therefore not due the good things in life. It came as no surprise when people treated me badly, rejected me, or said unkind things. All of that matched up with my expectations for myself.

Of course, I didn't own up to any of this at the time. I pretended more confidence than I felt, I told my parents my life was great, and I convinced my friends that the choices I made in dating and in big life decisions were truly choices and not surrender to the inevitability of a failed life. Precisely, I thought, what was due to a fat, ugly girl.

I created the life I thought I deserved. I married too young a man, who didn't love me and who was in many ways a cruel man. He told me every day that I was fat and ugly. I know looking back and with the knowledge I now have about the dynamics of control that his words were meant to keep me in line and that he may or may not have believed them. The words he used were tools or weapons, not meant to convey truth or feeling, and they worked. I dared not challenge him because I knew I deserved no better.

Looking back now from this vantage point that rests on many years of the hard work of personal growth and healing, as well as the foundation of being loved and seen by honest people with sincere goodwill, I wonder at how willing my younger self was to accept those definitions of herself and to reject her good qualities because she felt she didn't measure up on a couple of superficial criteria, criteria that now I wouldn't even recognize as valid. Good bodies are all different shapes and sizes, and beauty is as variable as we humans are.

I can only say that in those days, for a female, appearance was a very big deal. I think it still is. Our primary job was to find a man, get married, and raise a family. It didn't really matter much if you were smart, or strong, or competent, or adventurous, or any other attribute if you couldn't find a man. Everything hinged on that. And *looks* was how you did it, along with some truly amorphous quality called a *good personality*. I recall that I wondered then what that was, who had one, and could I copy it. Like much of adolescent skill, I never figured that out.

So I married the man who would have me and settled in to live whatever life he wanted to give me. It wasn't the worst. We lived in nice homes, he went to work every day, he paid the bills, he never put me in the hospital, and we showed up for family gatherings. My children got Halloween costumes and Christmas gifts and slept every night in warm beds. I was safe from all but verbal abuse, so long as I didn't challenge him or talk back or try to do anything on my own. Nothing could protect me from his cruel words, but then I believed them to be true and didn't even know them to be abuse. I just knew they hurt.

It also hurt that my young husband often stayed out all night, returning at daylight still drunk and stinking of the night's escapades, whatever they were. I honestly tried to suppress my pain and fury— but even fear couldn't contain it entirely. That's when he would hit me. And then he would tell me that it was my fault. My fault that he stayed out all night, that he had to drink, and that he hit me. My fault because I was a bitch and a nag and because I was a fat, ugly girl.

And I believed him.

When I looked in the mirror, I saw the woman he saw, and I stayed because that was all I deserved.

It was during this time that I first sought psychotherapy, and I've told that story in chapter 1. What matters here about that is that somehow in that brief experience, I was seen a little differently by someone who, for some reason, I trusted. He actually said to me that I was a "reasonably attractive woman." A modest compliment, for sure, but profound for me, a big step up from fat and ugly. Nothing dramatic happened after that. I didn't all of a sudden see myself differently, but I believe that the mirror cracked.

Eventually I left that marriage from fear that if I stayed, I would die, either because he killed me or because I could no longer live. Leaving didn't heal me. More years, more injuries, and much more work would be needed to heal my wounded sense of self. The process was gradual and uneven and fraught with danger. I got lost a lot and needed mountains of help to see it through. But bit by bit, I learned to see myself more clearly, to know of my beauty and its source, and to know that I, and others, see what we can see at any moment in time and only that. I also learned that being seen clearly and through the eyes of love is the crucial ingredient for people to heal and to begin to become who they were meant to be.

That young woman on the beach in the photo had much to learn and a long road to travel, but I recognize her. She's with me every day. She's the lingering self-doubt, but she's also the one who is brave enough and determined enough to keep trying, to move forward into the future, flaws and all. I never want to forget what she gave me and gives me still.

Sometimes it is necessary to reteach a thing its loveliness . . . until it flowers again from within, of self-blessing.

—Galway Kinnell, Pulitzer Prize–winning American poet

THIS THING ONLY

I too am born and grown to be this thing only;
to be Anna in the world.

—Anna Rydstedt-Dannstedt, Swedish poet

The young woman who entered my consultation room looked utterly defeated despite her almost breathtaking beauty. She was blonde, with the softest brown eyes I'd ever seen, tall, graceful, and somehow elegant even dressed as she was in an oversize sweatshirt and jeans. She said nothing. I indicated she should sit in the companion chair to mine, and she did, still saying nothing.

I began as I usually did with a new client by saying, "Hello, welcome, and what has brought you in to see me today?" She did answer then, saying that she was in treatment at a nearby residential substance abuse treatment program—she called it by name—and her therapist there referred her. I asked the reason for the referral, and she said, "I don't know. She thought I needed more," her eyes firmly averted from my gaze.

I asked if she had questions for me or if she would like to start by sharing some of her concerns with me. She bowed her head, looking now at the floor, and said softly, "I don't want to talk."

Now, you see, I do talk therapy. That's what we do; we talk and we talk, and from all this talking, somehow the clients eventually—sometimes sooner, sometimes later—hear themselves say precisely what they needed to hear and they are changed by that, and this change opens the door to possibility. And here I sit with this lovely human being who clearly is in great pain who says that she doesn't want to talk. What am I to do?

My training emphasized that it was important that most of the talking in session be done by the client, not me. Indeed, one of the indices that I use to monitor how the therapy is going is to notice how much I talk. Too much and something is awry. That's a sign that I need to back up and pay attention and let myself wonder and experience and follow where the client leads. They never taught me what to do when a client refuses to talk. I began to hear voices in my head with suggestions for what to do next. One of them said, "Well, just tell her that talking is what we do here." Another said, "Well, she won't be appropriate for therapy then." Yet another shouted, "Holy crap; what do you do now?" And another, "It won't hurt to wait a bit and see what happens."

I decided to follow the advice of that last voice and wait and experience and pay attention and wonder. So that's what I did. I told her that our time together was for her to use as she wished and that if she wanted to talk, that was fine, but that I was also willing to sit quietly with her. The hour passed, and as we neared the ending time, I said that I had at her counselor's request reserved a weekly hour for her, and I gave her the time set for her next appointment. I asked if she thought she wanted to keep that time. She nodded and left.

I saw a few more clients that day and managed to keep my focus where it belonged, but when the workday ended, I began to think about the young woman who refused to talk. I racked my mind for any tidbits of learning or training that might help me know how best to help her. The clinical team from her treatment program had provided medical records that themselves told quite a story. The client's name was Sara, and she was twenty-two years old, single, never married, and until recently a student at a prestigious university. After making perfect grades for three years, she had suddenly dropped out and entered treatment voluntarily for alcohol abuse. She had told the admissions team that she was drinking to intoxication daily, suffering blackouts, and that she feared for her life if she continued.

After detoxification, she began the therapy program at the center. Their records indicated that she had been previously treated for bulimia and had suffered several depressive episodes over the course of her adolescence and high school years. Despite that, she was an honor student, involved in campus activities, sports, and community service, and was elected homecoming queen her senior year. College admission committees were justifiably impressed with her record, and she had her choice of several impressive schools.

She came from a well-to-do family who lived in a lovely home in a nice neighborhood in a charming mid-size city in the Midwest. Her parents were good people who loved her. The family therapist who met with them had recorded his observations that perhaps the father was a bit rigid and the mother a little too much friend rather than parent, but overall he thought it was a stable and positive home environment.

Over the course of her treatment, which at this time was three weeks along, Sara had been compliant with clinical team recommendations and appeared to be safely withdrawn from the alcohol. However, staff members noted that her participation in groups was minimal and that she appeared isolated from other members of the patient community. She attended all groups and never caused problems, but the team worried that she was not using treatment to full effect. A consultation with a psychiatrist had resulted in a diagnosis of major depression, and he prescribed an SSRI antidepressant drug. She had been referred to me for individual therapy by the treatment team because they worried that their group modalities might not be sufficient for her needs.

Oh, I thought, I hope we don't fail her. I could see that on some level, everyone involved in her treatment felt that same way. Now, I don't want to criticize or to devalue in any way the extraordinary good that addiction treatment programs do, but it's tough work and often discouraging, and sometimes the people who work in these places fall into a pattern of blaming the patients when treatment fails. The most common symptom of this is when they start saying that the treatment failed because the patient wasn't sufficiently motivated. Of course, the truth is that their job is to help the patients discover their personal motives for change and that, if they could do that on their own, they wouldn't need the treatment team for much more than detoxification.

So I feared that Sara might fall into that crack if the pattern continued or that she might simply complete the recommended course compliantly and "graduate" and perhaps even stay sober, but not find the answers to the questions that had clearly been with her for years. So even though I didn't know quite how to proceed, I did know that I wanted to be of assistance to her if I could and that I would try my best to do that if she would let me.

She arrived on time for her next appointment, came in, sat down, and stared at the floor for fifty minutes. I simply told her that I was glad she came and that if she wanted to talk I wanted to listen, but that I was willing again to sit with her if that was her choice. The voices in my head had a grand old time with this, and I listened to them rant and rave while also listening to the sound of the silence in the room. This silence contained all the pain that Sara had been carrying with her for years and that she was still unable to speak about. On some level, I understood that. I too have known unspeakable pain, but my choice was always to talk as a way to hide it, to talk as a way to keep others from knowing—and myself as well. I began to think that Sara was very honest and very brave to say so clearly that she would not speak until the way was clear to speak her truth.

Three more times we did this. And on the sixth visit, she raised her head, looked me directly in the eye, and said, "I am gay." And I said, "All right. Is there something I can help you with?" She responded, "Yes, help me figure out how to tell my parents." And that was that, and we did, and they loved her anyway. And she went back to school and shone and became a brilliant scientist and has loved a woman now for many years and been loved in return, and the world is better because she was courageous enough to pledge to be *this thing only,* to be herself in the world, not some other person she thought—no, knew—the world wanted her to be, but simply herself.

As for me, I'm glad I didn't let my training get in the way of being present for this. I surely did want to be a good therapist and I do indeed value the methods and skills I was given, but people are so much more than that. As a therapist, that's the most important thing I've learned.

But as a therapist, I know that though the patient learns, I do not teach.

—Sheldon B. Kopp, American psychotherapist and author

8

AN INTERESTING LIFE

I am persuaded that the chief goal of the second half of life, and that of therapy by the way, is to make one's life as interesting as possible. That seems a modest claim, especially for a person in deep pain, yet our lives are an unfolding mystery, only partly in our control, in which we are not only the protagonist, but often the most amazed of witnesses.

—James Hollis, American author and Jungian analyst

People are so interesting. And so many of them don't know that. Of course, there are those who believe that they are the most incredibly interesting people alive. I once met a man who told me that he finally understood his problem: It wasn't that he thought too much of himself, but that he thought of himself too much. I liked that, and I really liked the way that simple idea helped him change his life, but I think the problem—if you can call it that—is not so much the quantity but the quality of one's self-thought.

One of the things I've noticed over the years is how much time people spend judging themselves. They think, "I'm too fat, I'm too lazy, I'm too short, I'm too stupid, I'm too messed up, I'm too _____"—fill in the blank with whatever quality seems to be required at the time. Everyday behavior gets the same sort of evaluation. Most of the people I meet are terribly hard on themselves.

This is a good time to talk about diagnosis. When people learn my profession, they typically have one of two reactions. The first is to say something along the lines of, "I'll have to be careful around you," which I guess assumes that I'm constantly on the alert for signs of emotional or mental disturbance. The second is some version of the sympathetic statement, "Oh, that must be very hard, hearing all those sad stories all day long." Of course, neither of those is anywhere close to the reality. With respect to the first, the truth is that when I'm not in the office, I rarely think in diagnostic terms—I'm far more likely to be caught in either the moment's experience or my own version of self-conscious reflection: Do I like this person, does this person like me, is my hair all right, and so on. As to the second reaction, it couldn't be further from the truth. My clients often do have sad, even tragic, stories, but they also have courage and perseverance and creativity and resilience, and what I learn from them every single day is hope.

As a clinician, I enjoy making diagnoses, and I'm very good at it. It's an endeavor that calls on rational analytical processes and often no small amount of detective work. I love puzzling through the often similar possibilities and arriving at a conclusion that can perhaps be helpful to the person. A good diagnosis leads to good treatment. An incorrect one can lead to treatment failure or to actual harm to the client. But here's the main thing to know about diagnosis: Whatever it turns out to be, and despite it or because of it, each individual is just that—an individual person, unique, precious, spectacularly himself or herself, and yet sharing the same yearnings, losses, fears, and longings of every other person. And every story, no matter how tragic or mundane, is inherently fascinating, full of challenges, successes, failures, missteps, and mysteries. It's a privilege to receive them. And I'm endlessly curious to learn how each of these particular people dealt with each thing that came their way, what they learned or didn't learn from it, and what happens next.

And when the clients develop that same curiosity about their own lives, regardless of the "diagnosis," they get better. Curiosity closes down judgment and opens the mind. Where there is curiosity, there is possibility. Without it, there is only either/or, good or bad, all or nothing, sick or well, broken or fixed, and we human beings are none of those things. Each of us is a mixed bag of this and that, bits and pieces, cloudy and clear. We never get fixed; we just go on repairing our brokenness and finding redemption within it. And we begin to do that the moment we get curious about our own lives.

The best way to begin is by telling your story. There are many ways to do that. You can journal, you can paint, you can talk to a friend, you can visit a priest or rabbi or other spiritual guide, or you can go to therapy. Just be sure that whoever you choose understands just how interesting you are. If they seem bored, move on to someone else. I'm not kidding. Run. But don't give up. Find someone who listens well and begin. What matters is that you make a start. You don't want to miss a minute of it. It's way too interesting to let it go past unnoticed.

Valmik: Let me tell you a secret: there is no such thing as an uninteresting life.

Maneck: Try mine.

Valmik: I would love to. One day you must tell me your full and complete story, unabridged and unexpurgated. You must. We will set aside some time for it, and meet. It's very important. . . .

Maneck smiled: Why is it important? . . .

Valmik: You don't know? It's extremely important because it helps to remind yourself of who you are. Then you can go forward, without fear of losing yourself in this ever-changing world. . . . Ah, yes, to share the story redeems everything.

—Rohinton Mistry, Indian-born Canadian novelist
(The quote is from pages 789–790 of his book,
A Fine Balance, Vintage International New York.)

9

CULTIVATING CURIOSITY

The guru instructs by metaphor and parable,
but the pilgrim learns through the telling of his own tale.

—Sheldon B. Kopp, American psychotherapist and author

One of the all-time best books ever written on psychotherapy was published in 1972 with the unlikely title *If You Meet the Buddha on the Road, Kill Him! The Pilgrimage of Psychotherapy Patients*. Its author, Sheldon B. Kopp, took the title from a Zen story meant to teach that the only good answers for any of us are our own answers and the journey of self-discovery is the quest to find within ourselves those answers that are good and true for us. Psychotherapy, for Kopp, is good psychotherapy when it aids in that process, rather than providing ready-made, one-size-fits-all solutions or, even, just treating the symptoms. The kind of psychotherapy suggested by Kopp assumes that the symptoms are a reflection of our not-knowing and they will disappear on their own when we know or, radically in our modern medical climate, weren't symptoms at all, but differences, either from the demands of the culture or our own expectations.

Cathy came to me with the stated desire to work through her feelings of loss and shame following a divorce. She and her former husband, Jeff, had married a few years out of college, with both their careers well established and youthful exploration done. She said that she expected to live her life with Jeff and grow old together and that the problems, when they developed, came as a complete surprise to her even though she felt the problems were mainly hers. She had grown impatient with qualities in Jeff she once admired and frustrated that he refused to change. The steadiness that attracted her became, in her eyes, boring. His calmness, a lack of feeling; his tenderness, weakness. She found herself drawn to other men and eventually into an affair. She had broken all her own rules and was profoundly disappointed in herself. And yet, she said she couldn't imagine staying with Jeff and felt the divorce was right for her. "I'm so confused. I don't know who I am anymore. I'm certainly not the person I thought I was, and I don't know if I even like the person I've become."

Cathy had not expected herself ever to be someone who could be driven by passion into irresponsible, hurtful behavior. She had not known that she could violate her own values. She didn't know that she was exactly like everyone else—strong and weak, brave and vulnerable, capable of great accomplishment and great failure. She thought she was one thing and turned out to be another, and she judged herself harshly.

It seems to me that all of us have two natures. One of these is our judging nature. We see a thing, we see ourselves, and we evaluate and judge what we see—good or bad, acceptable or unacceptable—and file it away in the right box and that's that. This nature comes in handy most of the time. It helps us know what to keep and what to let go, what to encourage and what to avoid, and to notice what needs changing.

Of course, it can go too far and, it seems to me, often does. Most of the people whom I've known as clients were powerful judges. No matter how crazy or wrong they might appear to the rest of the world, they themselves were their own harshest critics. While the public or family and friends might call them problems, they called themselves catastrophes. While others might see their sins as venial, they see them as mortal. Judgment is final, and the sentence is harsh—a lifetime of regret and self-loathing.

Seldom does a client openly acknowledge this state of affairs. Of course, they couldn't be aware of it in the way that I've expressed it, as an abstraction. For the client, for Cathy, this notion of a judging nature at work isn't a reality at all. For her, the reality is that she's discovered and been dismayed by a darker side to herself, and she doesn't know if she can live with that knowledge. For Cathy, this is crushing. Abstractions be damned, she's learned she isn't a good person after all, and how is she to go forward from there?

There's only one cure, and it's to be found in our other nature, curiosity. When confronted with new information of any kind, our curious nature's natural response is to want to know more about it, to ask questions, to do research, to study and reflect, and to understand.

So what I do, what seems to help, is ask questions. I ask how, and who, and when, and what, and, why? I ask and ask and ask again, until the client starts to ask himself or herself, and the questions lead to answers that expand self-awareness and evoke more questions; the answers aren't alibis or excuses, but clues and signposts that move us farther along the path of being human and making our journey, that move us toward understanding.

While we were together, Cathy only partially answered the whys and hows for the things she had done that led to the end of her marriage. She decided she didn't need to know all the answers, that she only needed to know that she was capable of great passion and great error and that she would need to stand guard and also stand ready with a forgiving spirit, because she was bound to both do her best and do wrong since that's the nature of creatures like us.

We need both sides of our dual natures. Judgment is critical to set the course and steady the travel. Without it, we fail to take the responsibilities that are rightfully ours and waste ourselves on blame and dependency. But judgment alone can't move us forward. Only our curious natures can do that.

If you met your Buddha and you followed him, you might find comfort in ready answers for a time, but ready answers may be false or fickle and lead to despondency when you inevitably fail to live up to their expectations or they fail to live up to yours. Even though we have much to learn from each other, only our own curiosity can pave the path to enlightenment.

Curiosity does, no less than devotion, pilgrims make.

—Abraham Cowley, English poet

10

OTHER PEOPLE'S BAD BEHAVIOR

A little kingdom I possess, where thoughts and feelings dwell;
And very hard the task I find of governing it well.

—Louisa May Alcott, American novelist and poet

I t was in the late 1990s, decades after my first attempt at psychotherapy and my failed first marriage and in a time when I had learned a great deal about myself and about life and when I was now happily married to a wonderful man, when I finally understood what it meant to be responsible for one's self. I remember the moment quite vividly, and it was a moment, a single instant in time, when everything thereafter was changed. Perhaps—almost certainly—there had been an unconscious process at work for some time that led to this moment, but I can only relay what happened and how it felt and what happened after that. I can't know what I don't know, and all I do know is that it came from nowhere and changed my life.

It happened in the South of France. I was walking in the village of Eze on the Mediterranean coast. Eze is an ancient town on a cliff fourteen hundred feet above sea level. Its history and situation define it. Old stone buildings line narrow cobbled streets that wind up and down the hillside. Any corner turned is as apt to reveal an exquisite view as to lead to a dead-end. One never knows. About three thousand people live here, so it's a true village, with a village sensibility. Well, at least a French museum village sensibility. People are friendly but reserved. They leave you to yourself unless invited. On this morning, not so early, but morning still, we had driven from Nice along

59

the Moyenne Corniche and parked in the lot at the bottom of the town and headed up. It's a sturdy little stroll to the top even when the pace is slow, so I was luxuriating in having achieved the summit. We stopped for coffee and a croissant, and I saw a shop I wanted to visit down the hill. My husband said he'd wait for me there and linger a bit with his caffe latte. So off I went to explore a bit on my own.

I don't know what I had been thinking about on the drive or during the walk up. Nothing of great importance, I'm sure. I love the South of France, and I'm usually content there. Ordinary worries don't seem to travel with me. But from somewhere and completely without preface came the thought: *Other people's bad behavior is no excuse for my bad behavior.* The thought literally stopped me in my tracks. First I thought, *Where did that come from and what's it about? What does it even mean? Could that be true? And if it is, what are its implications?*

Well, you see, there's the thing. The implications are momentous. If other people's bad behavior is no excuse for mine, then what is? Of course, the answer is nothing. There is no excuse for my bad behavior whatever forms it takes. No excuse at all. Bad behavior is just bad behavior. It stands alone and demands that it be viewed in its own light. I can try all I want to blame others for what I've done, but it won't hold because it isn't true, and in the deepest parts of myself, I know that. We all do, and finding it intolerable, we set out to excuse ourselves and somehow make it right by finding someone to blame. In the course of growing up and into ourselves, we all have to come to this moment. So long as we blame others or excuse our bad acts based on an external factor, we are prohibited from moving forward. Blame builds a wall, impenetrable and forever blocking the path to wholeness.

Accepting responsibility is profoundly liberating. We become free to choose whether to continue the behavior or not, whether to perpetuate the cycle or take steps in a different direction. We are empowered in the exact moment and to the exact extent that we own what's ours to own. I was short with the server yesterday because I was irritable and chose to express it, not because she was slow in her service. She was, but that belongs to her, and she has to own that. I was short because I chose to be: I know that since I have made the other choice on many occasions. This pretty young woman with the large goddess tattoo on her arm and her hair of many colors wasn't the first server to give me bad service. She wasn't the worst. I didn't dislike her; in fact, I thought she was beautiful and interesting, and I sort of wanted to know her. But I was frustrated about a project I couldn't seem to complete, my friend was sick, and I didn't sleep well that night, so I let my irritation at life in general and my fatigue dominate my actions. And I felt terrible after.

Bad behavior always leaves us with remorse, although we may barely notice it because we have become so skilled at ignoring our feelings or changing them so rapidly with this excuse or that alibi that the feeling quite literally goes unfelt in consciousness. But for better or worse, that doesn't mean it is really gone. No, not gone, but buried deeply with all the masses of tiny bad feelings that gradually and incrementally erode our self-respect. Negative messages from the outside world are not the only or even the most significant destroyers of self-acceptance. Far worse and far more common are the nearly imperceptible instances when we let ourselves down. We either behave in ways that we feel ashamed of, or we fail to stand for ourselves when we should. These self-denials each take a tiny little bit of our dignity, our confidence, our esteem, and over time become our self-image. I am someone who treats people badly and who isn't brave enough or strong enough to stop it. I am not someone I like.

And because that is intolerable, we work harder at making excuses and finding people to blame. And it's pretty easy to do. The world can be difficult to navigate, and other people and institutions are often wrong. So with minimal effort, in a flash, I can usually find someone to put it off on. And when I do, I get a bit of relief from the momentary anxiety. Whew! It's not me—it's them. They started it. I'm just the innocent victim here. I would never have done it if they hadn't . . .

Of course it sounds childish. It is. The part of me that needs to blame is the part that hasn't grown up. Because growing up always means taking responsibility. Always. To the extent that I am not taking responsibility, I am not grown up, no matter my age.

Not so very long ago, I came home from a social engagement feeling oddly disconnected and dissatisfied. I had enjoyed the event and spent time with people I like, so I couldn't quite understand my mood. At first, I ignored it, thought I might just be tired, but as I dressed for bed, I recalled a brief conversation with a friend that was basically gossip. We were both guilty of talking badly (despite it being dressed up in socially acceptable language and the proper amount of self-deprecation) about someone we knew. Now, the person in question had committed an offense against me, with concrete negative consequences for my life. Indisputable. But the fact was, it was long over, telling this other woman who knew nothing about it served no valuable purpose for anyone, and my motive was to assure that the person I liked didn't hold my offender in high regard. Gossip, plain and simple. My first thought was that it was deserved, my second thought was that my friend was glad enough to join in, and my third thought was, never mind, it was still gossip and that's not who I want to be. No wonder I felt bad.

In the past, before I knew that other people's bad behavior was no excuse for mine, I would have stopped with the first or second thought, and my bad feeling would have buried itself and added itself to a thousand, million, billion others and become part of my sense of myself. But the knowledge I gained in that moment in the village of Eze, now also part of who I am, gave me the freedom to accept my responsibility and decide what to do about it. In this case, I decided to redouble my efforts to guard against gossip and, at the first opportunity, to apologize to my friend for pulling her into that little gossip session.

Yes, I am someone who is tempted to gossip sometimes. I don't like it; I plan to keep on building that aspect of my character to the best of my ability day by day. Awareness will help me do that. I am likely to err from time to time, and when I do, I'll do what I can to correct it. Make no mistake. I choose me. I don't care much for this failing of mine and I hope to make it better, but I don't love myself any less and I won't stop being my own friend. I won't give up on me. I choose me, even the part that gossips. It's only in choosing and owning that I am free to change.

God did not make us to be eaten up by anxiety, but to walk erect, free, unafraid in a world where there is work to do, truth to seek, love to give and win.

—Joseph Fort Newton, American clergyman and author

11

GETTING BIGGER

*When I stand before thee at the day's end, thou shalt see my scars
and know that I had my wounds and also my healing.*

—Rabindranath Tagore, Indian poet, philosopher,
and winner of the Nobel Prize for Literature in 1913

After three decades of doing therapy and even more decades of living life, I've finally begun to understand what people need in order to first, heal, and then flourish. Of course, it's not what I thought at all. I thought we needed "the answers" or "the secret." So much of it, the pathway to happiness or wholeness or centeredness or whatever word currently represented the state we all seek, seemed elusive and even unobtainable. I wanted, hoped, to be cured or fixed and to be able to give that to others.

Here's what I've finally learned. We don't get cured or fixed. We don't even get better. What we do is get bigger. We grow ourselves into someone who can do what we could not do before: cope, forgive, encompass, ask, give, love, hope, succeed, who doesn't need whatever it was that got us by before and was killing us in the process.

The essential question is no longer how can I get rid of this symptom or change this habit or even feel better? The question has become, in what way can I enlarge myself and my life that will move this process forward?

For me at least, this shift in thinking is revolutionary. It totally replaces the system I was operating from before. I spent many, many years trying to fix me, not knowing that I wasn't broken at all, just too small to carry the energies demanding my attention. I didn't know

65

myself well enough or understand enough about life to be able to manage outer circumstances and sustain inner balance.

Nothing needed repair, and equally, nothing could be repaired. What is, is. Where I'm wounded, the scars will remain. My losses can't be undone. My mistakes and misdeeds can't be retracted. My failures stand. Which, it turns out, is perfectly fine, because all of them can be made valuable by enlarging my understanding and often my activity. If I am depressed, it's because I don't currently have sufficient hope, love, and grace in my life. If I am angry, my task is not to get rid of the anger; my task is to find more acceptance or more forgiveness, or to grow myself into someone who sets better limits. Not different, just bigger.

I don't need to get rid of something to be happy or whole; I need to add something. And that's where the work is. And it's very, very hard, but it is possible. The problem with my old method is that, in the end, it was an impossible task. You can't fix what isn't broken, and you can't undo what's already been done. You can, however, find a way to encompass it, to hold it, to claim it, and in so doing, redeem it. When I find a way to enlarge my understanding, my life, or my spirit, I make room for the events and themes that have shaped me and transform them from harm to power, from injury to resource, from loss to lesson.

On the surface, this idea may seem too simple, like yet another quick fix or platitude in a world awash with both. Trust me, this work is neither simple nor quick. It requires delicacy, diligence, and often quite a lot of time. Whatever wounds we carry or shortcomings we currently display, they took time to develop, and they will fight us tooth and nail to maintain their control.

Our commitment to our woundedness can be astonishingly profound. While part of us desperately longs for relief from the pain, another part holds tightly to the familiarity and the sense of connection the wound represents. So long as I am wounded, I am still connected to the source of the wound. If I let go, what will be left? And if I let go of my shortcomings, how would I cope? Would I be the same person? Those are frightening questions indeed to one who has lost faith in the future or in themselves, and since the questions are often operating outside the reach of consciousness, their hegemony is absolute until we expose them and answer them. We must develop sufficient courage and stamina to face those questions and answer them in the only way we can, which is to say, "I don't know the answers, but I am willing from here forward to risk not knowing and allow the answers to come in their own time."

You see how difficult this is. Only the very brave and the very faithful can make the journey. Fortunately, we all have the potential to be that brave and that faithful with the right kind of assistance from ourselves and sometimes from others.

The quest for the better life is a multibillion-dollar industry precisely because we are all seekers. On this journey of life, we go in search of answers to our fundamental questions of belonging, of identity, and of meaningfulness, and we hope against hope that someone will have the answers for us. We turn to this guru or that diet or the latest self-help book's "secret" formula, and they sometimes help, but most often we regain the weight or slide back into old patterns or become disillusioned with the guru's advice. We may blame ourselves or become more disaffected. The problem, though, rests not in the fallibility of gurus or the motives of the diet industry. Nor can we reasonably blame ourselves. It's just part of the human condition that we don't know what we don't know until we know it, and we are all hoping for similar things—happiness, success in whatever form, connection, meaningfulness, a sense that we matter in the bigger scheme of things. We go out looking for these things, and often we are mistaken or misguided.

It may also be part of the human condition that many of our questions will remain unanswered and that we will remain imperfect throughout our lifetime. I can't find any record of any human achieving perfect knowledge or perfection of spirit in a single lifetime. But there is a path to be taken that leads to greater self-awareness, an enlargement of spirit, and a more peaceful relationship with life. Most of us find it at some point along the way by intention or by accident. My own experience includes both deliberate self-improvement and unsought discoveries. I have come to believe that the key is simply to keep moving and keep trying and that what was impossible becomes possible, incrementally or suddenly, and that, yes, time is the great healer.

Still, when I encounter new challenges, part of me hopes that someone will provide me with a formula or list of guidelines for how to meet them. In my case right now, I'm longing for an accurate and truthful guide to thriving in old age or even just a reasonably effective program for dealing with joint pain. Some of you want "rules for success in . . ."—business, marriage, finding the right man/woman, losing weight, living a happy life, and so forth. And, Lordy, there are plenty of people out there willing to provide just that, and many of them have some good things to say. You just have to keep in mind that they are all only partially correct or offer one possible answer among many, or maybe they are not at all correct for you because you are you and not that other person. You don't need a guru. You only need to locate within yourself that point of growth and find ways to nourish it. You don't need to be fixed because you aren't broken. You are in the process of growing up, and if you've noticed a problem or a challenge, that means it's time for that to move toward integration.

And you yourself must move it forward. No one can do that for you. You are responsible for you, and you are the expert on you. Listen carefully to others and make your own decisions. We each must find our own particular path to our very best, and each of us is much bigger than we know we are. There is room for everything, everything we are and everything that has happened so far in these lives we are creating.

Every blade of grass has its angel that bends over it and whispers, "Grow, grow."

—The Talmud

PART II

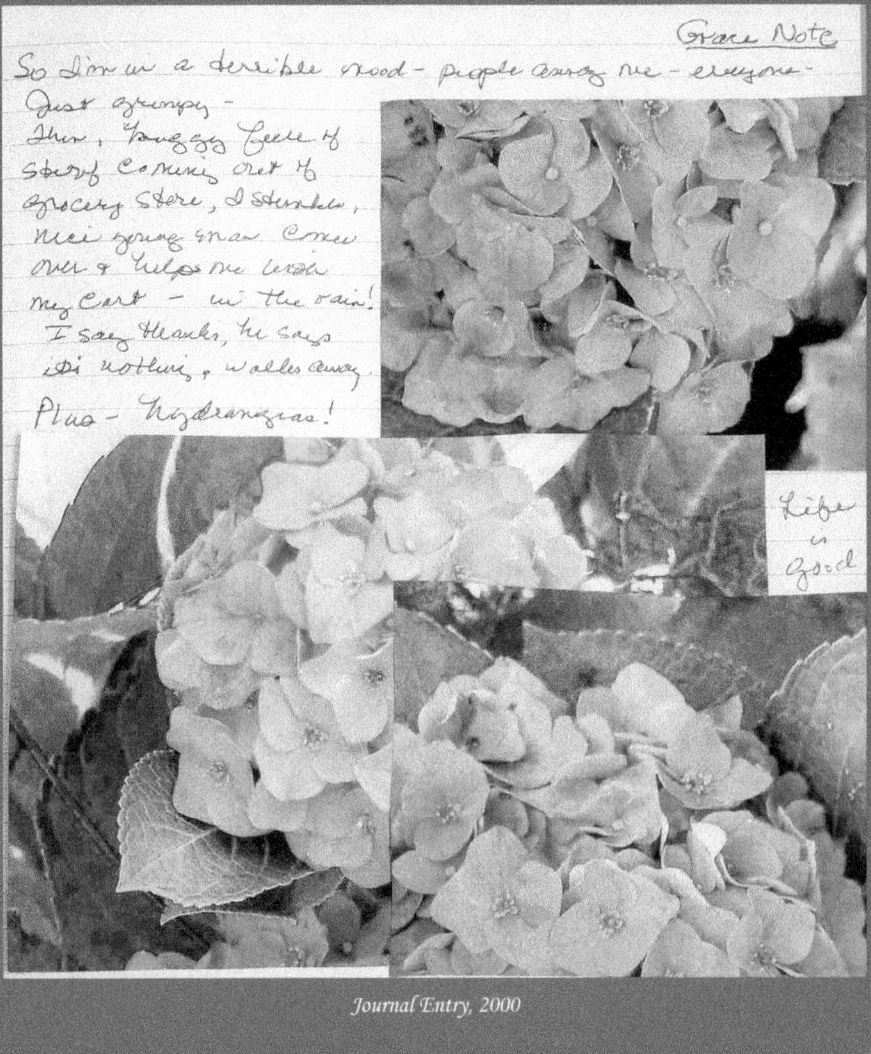

Journal Entry, 2000

REDEMPTION

Redemption: the act of making something better or more acceptable; the act of exchanging something for money, an award, etc.; the act of saving people from sin and evil.

—*Merriam-Webster Dictionary*

I didn't know when I made my first therapy appointment that I was seeking wholeness or that its path was largely founded on self-awareness. I went in hopes of feeling better, and I thought that if I could find out what was wrong with me, I would be able to fix it, or someone would, and then I could be happy or at least free of misery. I didn't think too much about the whole question of how just talking to someone might enable me to find relief, but if I had, I think I might have found it unlikely in the extreme. I've heard that question from many clients over the years, and I've understood their skepticism. How can it be that going to an office and sitting and talking with someone, no matter how kind or skilled, can relieve this horrible pain that I've carried for years? What can he or she possibly say to make me feel better?

Therapy works, when it does, because the client is able to discover his or her own truth and place it in a context that can hold and sustain and empower it to create the foundation for the unfolding future. Self-awareness is the starting place. In order to grow and become and thrive, it's necessary to begin where we are, and we can't do that until we get to know ourselves. That often means trudging back through time and confronting previously denied, distorted, or repressed thoughts, feelings, events, and relations. This work is hard, can take months or years, and may at times seem unbearably painful or even pointless.

And yet, more often than not, it works. People get better because they show up and tell their stories and someone listens, and slowly, gradually, judgment gives way to curiosity and the abandoned self is reclaimed and renewed through greater understanding. Old structures fall away, to be replaced with clarity and compassion, first for self and inevitably for others as well.

Therapy, then, as well as other paths to wholeness, can genuinely be considered a process of redemption, the act of making something better or of being saved from "sin and evil." We can't move forward in our lives nor can we cherish the present moment when the contents of the past are shaping our experience. Nor can we pretend or deny or ignore or repress or forget without consequences for the present. Whatever lurks in the shadows of our past and in the recesses of our psyches needs to be faced head on, healed, and transformed.

If I am to have any hope of wholeness, then everything, absolutely everything, that has gone before must be redeemed. I must get to know the story I've been living and decide how it needs revision. I must rediscover all the alienated aspects of self, my disconnections, distorted perceptions, and denied qualities. I need to go back and revisit the trajectory of my life up to now—every wound, injury, disgrace, and rejection I've suffered and every lie, theft, injustice, and misdeed that I've committed. I must get honest with myself and own up to my shortcomings and misconduct and find a way to forgive myself. I must also find a way to forgive everyone else as well, no matter how egregious their actions. Otherwise I carry that wound forward and with it contaminate my present and my future.

To forgive is not to condone, whether the forgiveness is for me or for the other. What's wrong is wrong, and all of us are guilty at times in our lives. Forgiveness recognizes the wrongness, and then chooses to move forward from it. Forgiveness judges the action, rather than the actor. Forgiveness relinquishes the stronghold we have on resentment and woundedness, so that we are free to move ahead.

Nor does forgiveness excuse. It may attempt to understand some of the reasons behind the action, but that doesn't turn those reasons into an alibi. Excuses and alibis become justifications for future wrongness. Reasons may aid understanding in ways that help us to avoid making the same mistakes again, whether in terms of our own behavior or in our relations with others.

Self-awareness opens the door, and the process of redeeming the past sets us firmly on the path. We are in some ways all of us lost souls in need of redemption. We may need to reclaim some of our deepest, purest longings, buried beneath layers of distortion and denial. We will surely need to learn to give attention to our lingering pain and loving support for our ongoing efforts to become our best selves.

Redemption is a word most often used in a religious context. But it applies here precisely because the process of growth and healing that comprises the journey to wholeness is a process of spiritual development, grand in its way and meaningful. No matter our religion or secular belief system, each of us has the birthright, and also the responsibility, to create the life we are meant to live. We weren't made for perfection; we were made for wholeness, and its realization is a lifelong and profoundly important journey. We each have a part to play and the opportunity to play our parts well, if only we are willing to endure and persist and continue reaching for clarity and compassion.

Seeking to forget makes exile all the longer; the secret of redemption lies in remembrance.

—Richard von Weizsäcker, German president, 1984–1994

12

PSYCHOTHERAPY 2
THE GURU

People take different roads seeking fulfillment and happiness. Just because they're not on your road doesn't mean they've gotten lost.

—Dalai Lama XIV, Tibetan Buddhist spiritual leader

About five years after my first psychotherapy experience, I tried again. This time, I made an appointment with a man who was locally famous for his breakthrough methods. Several people said, "Oh, you have to go to George—he is THE BEST." Their voices did seem to capitalize the letters when they said that. I told him on the phone that I thought I wanted to try group therapy. I have always read a lot, and I had been reading the new books and magazine articles about the success people were having with the new group modalities—so much better and quicker than the dominant model of psychoanalysis, with the therapist/doctor, the patient on the couch, and three to five visits per week for years.

George told me we would need to meet individually for an assessment and to determine which, if any, of his groups I might fit into. I agreed, and we set the day and time. As before, I planned to keep this venture secret from my husband, who would have objected and who had become, if anything, even more determined to maintain tight control of all the elements of his life. However, my career had advanced, and my position offered much more autonomy as well as enough money that this expense would not be immediately missed. I felt a bit less of a thief, and I had long since decided that keeping secrets from my husband was just going to be a fact of my life.

In keeping with this shift in therapy modes, the office this time was located in an old house in the city's burgeoning upscale shopping district, where residential neighborhoods were rapidly becoming commercial districts. This house was between an expensive and oh-so-charming restaurant and an exclusive hair salon, both of which also occupied former homes. The waiting room had been a living room, and I'm sure George's office was the master bedroom at one time, but now it housed the same sort of desks, bookcases, and chairs that filled my first therapist's office. The differences were in the light and the color. There were windows on two sides of the room, blinds open to the natural world, and furnishings tended toward tribal art, Navajo rugs, and multihued pillows on couches and on the floor.

I knew immediately that I was out of my league, that this man was far more sophisticated and urbane than I was or would ever be. Nevertheless, I entered, we talked, and he told me that (a) I was not very emotionally available, (b) I was not "ready" for group therapy without undergoing individual therapy beforehand, and (c) I could join his group that met on Wednesday evenings at seven. I'm not at all sure how we moved from (b) to (c)—I can only imagine that there were intervening words that somehow bridged that gap, but I recall only those three things.

I also don't recall how I managed to attend the group sessions I attended without giving away my secret. I know that it was exceedingly rare for me to do anything on my own in the evening and that I would have needed babysitting for my two daughters. I guess I must have told lies about Tupperware parties or baby showers, but from this distance, that seems too flimsy a shield, one surely to be seen through with almost no effort at all. Funny how the mind works to sort and edit what it stores and where and when we can access it. Perhaps I'll recall all this later, but it's not available now.

Anyway, I attended the group three times. There were nine of us: five women, three men, and George. The first night, after each group member had checked in with a report on how their week had been and what they wanted to talk about in group, one of the women made her way on to the floor and began to scream and moan; George joined her and, in the end, held her in his arms and rocked her. The group sat silently through this, but at the end, they all told her "great work." I may have said something, but what I thought was that either these people were all crazy or else there was something really seriously wrong with me. I honestly thought she was faking, and if she wasn't, she needed more help than she was going to get in that group or she just needed to learn to contain herself.

I went back the next week. That night's session was less dramatic, but one of the men talked for a long time about his father's unrealistic expectations and how damaging they were to his sense of himself and to his virility. I had never heard a man talk about his sexual performance. I was shocked and secretly felt again that he should keep that stuff to himself. Others talked, and my reactions varied from sympathy to curiosity to annoyance, but never identification.

The third week, George said it was time I shared with the group some of my concerns. My stomach dropped. I was terrified of these people. And it turns out, rightly so. When I told them that I was there because I was unhappy in my marriage and thinking of a divorce, they attacked me. Now perhaps George or one of the other group members would describe what happened differently, but what happened to me, since I perceived it that way, was that I was attacked. They told me I had no right to sit there in their group for two weeks and not provide them with that information, that I was dishonest and they would have a hard time trusting me going forward. I cried. I mean I really cried. I could not stop. These painful remarks continued, some harsher than others. I felt a hand take mine, and I believe that hand kept me from coming completely undone. I didn't know the owner of that hand—she was just the woman sitting to my left.

That's where the group ended, with me crying and they just walked out and left me like that. I got my bag and made my way to my car. No one asked if I was okay to drive. No one asked anything.

I didn't go back.

I don't know what I made of all this. I remember feeling dreadful for days afterward, too ashamed to talk about it, almost too ashamed to think about it. I knew that these educated, sophisticated people understood something I didn't and that it must be something everyone knew but me since no one felt a need to teach me about it. I leapt in my mind back and forth between defending myself and blaming them and then back again to plain old despair. Mostly I was profoundly confused. Why was it bad that I didn't tell them before? I honestly didn't know that was the kind of thing you talked about or even if it was my turn to talk.

George had been right. I was not ready for group therapy; I wish he could have helped me, but he didn't. Indeed, the whole experience left me feeling more alone and diminished in some significant way.

I did get my divorce. It was an excruciating time in my life. My husband threatened to kill me one day and pleaded with me to stay the next. He said that I would never find another man to love me—"Who would want a woman like you? Who would want a woman with two children in tow? Who could possibly love you except me?"

I didn't know the answer to any of those questions. I just knew I had to go and that whatever happened and wherever I found myself would be preferable. I knew that he didn't love me no matter what he said. I knew I didn't love him even if maybe I had at one time. I knew that I didn't know what love looked like or even if it existed, but that I had to try to find out. I didn't like the woman I was and I didn't know if I could be another sort of woman, but I knew I had to try.

I went to George looking for a kind of redemption and a kind of love. I didn't know that's what I was looking for or where to find either, but my culture said people like me often found answers in therapy. I'm sure they did, but I didn't then. I've wondered from time to time what might have happened if I'd had a different experience, if I'd chosen a less cutting-edge, fashionable sort of guru to be my guide.

But that's what happened, and what matters more is what happened next. What happened was that I took the next step, and the next step is the holy step because that's how we walk, one step at a time, into our future selves. I didn't find redemption with my second attempt at therapy, but I did move the process forward, and I learned a little more about the world and, in an odd sort of way, what love looks like. I learned it's not found in grandiosity or drama or in words of any kind. I learned that it doesn't leave you bereft, with not even a voice of encouragement. I learned that sometimes it's just a stranger's hand holding yours and that sometimes it looks more like courage.

I didn't get redemption then, but I believe I've been able to redeem that part of my life. I've learned to look more kindly on that lost and confused woman. I was in fact unloved then. Circumstances and my own defenses assured that I would be. I didn't know how to change that then, but I can smile at my determination to keep trying until I found a way. Knowing all that I know now, I can even smile a bit at George, caught up in his new ideas and newfound fame and probably certain that his way was the helpful one. After all, I've learned that we therapists are just fellow travelers, as subject to human vulnerability and to the ambiguities of life as anyone else. What we can and must offer, however, is the form of love found in honest communication, adherence to boundaries, respect for personhood, and the commitment to be present and listen actively and purposefully to the stories our clients bring, carefully honoring the client's pace and place with patience and sensitivity.

One is not born, but rather becomes, a woman.

—Simone de Beauvoir, French writer and existentialist philosopher

13

PSYCHOTHERAPY 3
THE STUDENT

Experience: that most brutal of teachers.
But you learn, my God, do you learn.

—C. S. Lewis, English author, academic, and Christian philosopher

My third attempt at psychotherapy came when I was in my early thirties and in graduate school. I knew that I was on a downward spiral, and I hoped someone could interrupt it because I knew that I could not. I didn't have anyone I could confide in except one lovely friend who assured me I was fine because that's how she always saw me. Still sees me. She's a beautiful, generous woman.

But she was wrong that time, and I was right. I needed help and I needed something to shift, but I truly did not know what or how. By this time, I had no money and no insurance. I had given up my job for full-time study, as required by my doctoral program. I had a fellowship that covered my tuition and provided a small stipend for my living expenses. I am now and was then grateful for this assistance, but it was barely sufficient for basic needs, so there were no funds for health care of any sort. Fortunately I was healthy and rarely needed to see a physician.

The school did offer counseling services through the student union on a sliding scale or free basis. The therapists there were doctoral candidates working under the supervision of a faculty member, a licensed clinician. So I made an appointment.

The therapist's name was Richard. He was about my age and seemed like a nice enough man. We had three sessions together. We spent them talking about the fact that he had recently learned his girlfriend had herpes and he didn't know if he would be able to stay with her under those circumstances and risk getting it himself.

I may have told him my concerns, but maybe not. I'm not sure he would have heard me if I did.

I hope he found his answers. I didn't, but I learned a lot from him. Thinking back, I believe that Richard may have shared his personal concerns with me in an attempt to give me confidence to share mine. I am convinced he was doing his best to help me. But I, at that time, only heard another version of what I already believed, that I didn't matter, even in this formal helping relationship. Later, when I sat in Richard's place in another therapy room, the memory of those sessions helped me keep the focus where it belonged and to remember that I don't know what a client needs until he or she has the ability and will to tell me. I learned to wait and listen.

There are no mistakes, no coincidences. All events are blessings given to us to learn from.

—Elisabeth Kübler-Ross, Swiss-American psychiatrist
and pioneer in the study of death and dying

14

THIMBLEFUL OF HOPE

Redemption just means you just make a change in your life and you try to do right, versus what you were doing, which was wrong.

—Ice T, American rapper and actor

Although I didn't know it then, my decision to go for therapy was an act of redemption. Intuitively, without understanding much about human nature or the journey of life and with virtually no insight to my own inner life, I knew that I could only move forward by redeeming what had gone before. I needed to know what was wrong with me and if it could be fixed. I needed to know if I had value and, if so, what that value rested in. I needed to know if I was lovable and capable of loving. I needed to be saved.

Years later, when I sat in the therapist's chair and other people sat across from me, I would recall my very first session as a client and the tightly bound fear and thimbleful of hope I brought in with me. Once a young man came to my consultation room, and one of the first things he said to me was, "I know you won't be able to help me." I understood that. I knew what it felt like to believe yourself to be beyond help, but to be carried forward anyway by that thimbleful of hope that maybe, just maybe, redemption was possible. I told him that he might be right, but that I was willing to try my best anyway. He got better—we found ways together to redeem what had been lost or find that which was hidden so that he could make a better life for himself.

His name was Ronnie, and he was the adopted son of older parents who had two other, older children. As he understood it, his birth mother and father had abandoned him, and this couple, who were his mother's relatives, had "taken him in." He told me how good they had been to him—kind, generous, and patient. "They treated me like one of their own kids," he said. But, he said, he was always a problem. He got into trouble at school; he acted out at home; he used drugs and alcohol, eventually earning legal problems as well. There were also health issues. He was diagnosed in early childhood with frontal lobe epilepsy, which worried his parents and necessitated frequent medical treatments and interventions, including surgical procedures and long hours of home nursing care. He was, he said, just one great big problem for everybody, including himself.

His reason for making the appointment to see a therapist on this day was that he needed someone to talk to and everyone he knew, he said, was tired of hearing his complaints. He had plenty. He was sure that his neighbors—at twenty-eight, he now lived alone in a small apartment, partially subsidized by disability income and partially by his father—were plotting to have him evicted. His father, who had been his most loyal supporter, never seemed to have time for him now. His mother wouldn't allow him in her home. One of his siblings still seemed friendly, but the other refused his calls. But by far, his main complaint was that he couldn't find a girlfriend. Most of the women he met were not appealing to him—"stupid or trampy"—and the ones he liked didn't like him. He had tried online dating, but no one would go out with him a second time. He thought he would be all right if he could just meet the right girl and settle down. Although he never used the word, he was telling me he was lonely and that he had come to me for companionship and to be heard, that what he wanted was a cure for his loneliness.

I was willing to do that. I thought he was correct, that what he needed was to be heard and eventually to be able to hear himself and learn what needed learning so that he could move out from where he was to where he wanted to go. He didn't know—and why would he?—that he would need to go back to what was lost before he could find the way forward. He needed to know the same things I had needed to know years before: he needed to know what was wrong with him and if it could be fixed. He needed to know if he had value and, if so, what that value rested in. He needed to know if he was lovable and capable of loving. He needed to be saved.

And he found his redemption the same way I did. Gradually, over time, little bits of love became little bits of healing. Thimbles full of hope produced courage to risk new things. The parts of himself that were hostage to the hurts and mistakes of the past were freed when the stories were told and the meanings revised in light of new understanding. A man hears a story in a different way than a child does. Slowly Ronnie found a way to become a friend to the child who first knew those stories and saw only people to blame. A man can hear about wrong things and find ways to understand and forgive. Understanding and forgiveness, each a form of love, when combined with right action, form the only reliable path to redemption.

We can never obtain peace in the outer world until we make peace with ourselves.

—Dalai Lama XIV, Tibetan Buddhist spiritual leader

15

PATIENCE

Patience is the art of hoping.
—Luc de Clapiers, eighteenth-century French writer and moralist

I was a freshly minted psychologist ten days into my new job in an acute psychiatric treatment facility when Bethanne was assigned to my caseload in our morning clinical staff meeting. I had learned already that the best source of information about patients was the nursing staff, so I listened carefully as the shift supervisor described the nurses' observations of this woman. She had been a patient for the better part of a month and had yet to leave her room except to use the toilet and that only infrequently. She never spoke or acknowledged the staff in any way. Despite the head nurse's efforts to be professional, I could also hear that the staff was becoming anxious and frustrated with Bethanne. Ours was an ambulatory unit, with the expectation that patients could be depended upon to take care of their personal needs and to eat meals in the dining room. Bethanne needed special attention, and the staff worked to their limits without this additional burden. Even housecleaning had complained about not being able to keep the room clean with her in her bed all day.

Our chief psychiatrist said that Bethanne had been diagnosed with major depressive disorder and that she had a history of multiple admissions for her illness, with a positive response to treatment, which in the past had consisted of psychopharmacological intervention combined with group therapy and supportive living guidance from the social work staff. Then, however, she had been more "cooperative," and they were considering transferring her to another facility that was better able to accommodate her current condition.

I asked what my role in her treatment would be, and the chief said I should try to get her to take a bath.

Normal procedure at that time was that I would check in with each of my assigned patients daily and have two half-hour sessions per week with each person. Check-ins were normally brief, and I might do them in my office or on the unit in a less formal manner. Sessions were held in my office with privacy assured, a rare thing on a psychiatric unit. I had never been in a patient room. But that day, I made my way to Bethanne's room, knocked, and received no response. Honestly, I had no idea what to do next, but I tentatively pushed the door open and, listening carefully for any acknowledgement—positive or negative—I entered the room. Not a sound emanated from her bed. I could see her there with the covers pulled to her chin and her head turned toward the wall. I stood near the door, introduced myself, and told her that I had come to chat with her and to see if I could be helpful in any way.

Nothing. I waited a bit and then walked over and sat in the straight-backed chair that stood by the small, barred window. Not knowing what to say, I said nothing.

After a little while, I stood and said that I would be back the next day and that I would check in each day to see how she was doing and, if she thought of any way I might be helpful to her or if she had anything she wanted to talk about, I would do my best to help.

The next day was a repeat of the first. I once again told her who I was in case she didn't remember and said I'd just wait a few minutes to see if she wanted to talk, and I did. I sat and waited for ten minutes or so, then told her I'd see her the next day. Occasionally I spoke about something—the weather or the sound of a bird outside her window. Once or twice I asked if she would like to take a bath, I think—those had been my instructions at any rate.

This continued for several days. I would arrive at the scheduled time, announce myself, and go sit quietly in the chair by the window. Although I was frightened the first time I entered her room and somewhat repelled by the musty smell that is inevitable in a room that's always occupied and poorly cleaned, after a few visits, I began to find a peacefulness in the quiet of her room. I felt her sadness as if it were an energy every bit as potent as sound or light, but along with the sadness, I could also almost understand the choice to stay under the covers rather than confront the possibility of coldness, indifference, or pain outside the room. I did not, of course, say that out loud. I just asked again if she might consider talking with me, and when she didn't reply, I said I'd be back again the next day.

I don't know if it was the eighth day or the ninth or tenth, but one day as I was sitting in the chair by the window, Bethanne said, "I want to get my hair done." I said, "OK. I'll make that happen. Would you like a bath as well?" She nodded and slid back under the blanket.

I did make it happen, she did take the bath, and by the third or fourth day later, she was coming to meals and keeping appointments with me in my office and sometimes even watching TV or playing cards with the other patients.

She told me she had backed herself into a corner that she didn't know how to get out of. She first went to bed because she felt so bad about herself that she wanted to "go away," but lacked the courage or the energy to actually run away, either in life or through death. The longer she stayed, the more impossible it was to get up. Finally, it boiled down to her hair. She simply couldn't imagine walking around among people with her hair in the condition she knew it had to be in after that long in bed. So she couldn't get up, and she couldn't ask to get her hair done. She didn't know us, and she felt that some of us didn't like her much.

She said she had noticed that I kept my hair nice, and so she thought I might understand. And you know what? She was right. I did understand. I know that when a thing is hard, it's even harder when you feel inferior or unacceptable. And I know that when a thing is hard, you need to feel as strong as possible to meet it. I also know that, for a woman, that strength sometimes comes from knowing you look your best or, at least, that your hair is done.

After a while, Bethanne left the hospital, and as is common practice in psychiatric institutions, she was referred to a community resource for follow-up, and I lost touch with her. I hope that she got what she needed to heal and grow and that she didn't need readmission. I will always be grateful to her for teaching me to sit still and wait and that, for most of us, it's the simple things that count the most. All my fancy education and all the skill of this exemplary psychiatric staff were completely useless to her. It turned out that what she needed most was patience and a little bit of understanding, and I could give that, not because I had them to start with, but because I learned them from her.

There have been many times since then when I have encountered a situation I didn't know how to handle, a resistance that I could not budge, in my practice and in my life. When I do, my initial reaction is usually to try harder, work harder, argue more effectively, push, pull, drag, somehow or other force the solution I want. It's exhausting for me and likely frustrating for whoever is on the other side or in the path. How much better it is when I can recall the chair under the window and how it felt to sit and wait and let the solution emerge in its own time and its own way.

I have just three things to teach: simplicity, patience, compassion. These three are your greatest treasures.

—Lao Tzu, ancient Chinese philosopher and founder of Taoism

16

REDEEMING THE PAST

To forgive is to assume a larger identity
than the person who was first hurt.

—David Whyte, English poet, author, and philosopher

aul came for his first session with me and announced, "I'm not here to talk about the past. There's nothing to talk about. It's over. One of the reasons I was reluctant to come is that I am not interested in blaming my parents for the problems in my life. I only want to talk about what's going on right now and get some solutions so I can go on with my life." I was no stranger to this attitude: I would say about half of my first-time-in-therapy clients make similar statements, so I nodded and said, "All right, perhaps then you could begin by telling me about those problems so we can get to work on their solutions."

I know, of course, that if we proceed with the work, we will encounter the past and much will be gained from the encounter. I was not being disingenuous in avoiding a direct response to his comments. Nothing would be gained by doing so, and in the deepest sense, the past is indeed never past. It is with us always, and therefore in a very real sense, every engagement with our history is an engagement with the person who exists right now in this moment and there is in fact no way to talk about ourselves that doesn't include bits and pieces of what went before, if only in what isn't said.

The Paul who came to me that day wanted to talk about current problems in his marriage. His wife of ten years had grown cold

91

toward him after the birth of their second child four years ago. He said he loved his wife and children and wanted to continue in the marriage, but needed a companion who was also his lover. He shyly admitted that his wife, Diane, was seldom interested in sex, and though this was painful to him, even more painful was her avoidance of any physical affection. Paul said he missed kissing and holding hands and snuggling together in front of the TV.

I asked him about the ways he had addressed the problem up to now, and he said he had tried talking to her, but she said she was too busy with the children and too tired at the end of the day. "She not only won't do it; she won't talk about it. " Diane had also refused his request that she accompany him to my office.

As you can see, Paul had firmly located the problem outside of himself, placing it instead squarely inside his wife. Now if this were truly where the problem lay, there would be precious little I could do to help. Since we can never change another person and she did not want to come, he and I were both helpless to solve the problem.

So, I basically told Paul that. I said, "Well, if that's the case, if indeed you've tried everything you know and Diane won't change or doesn't want what you want and she doesn't want to work on it with you, there's little I can do to help. There may be one thing we could do together if you are willing. We could explore together the ways that you are approaching Diane and see if perhaps there's some hidden aspect that interferes with your connection. But only if you feel it might prove helpful."

He responded, "I'm not sure, but we'll try it for a few sessions."

Of course, then I asked him to tell me his life story. And with no resistance at all, he did. His healing began right then because several things happened when he made that choice. He reclaimed part of the current problem, if only unconsciously, and he also began the process of awakening, to know himself more clearly and more deeply. He opened the door for his journey of self-discovery and took his first tentative steps along the path.

What we learned together was that he carried with him the expectation of sexual and affectionate rejection and that the origins of that expectation were located precisely where he did not at first wish to travel—in the past. He learned, too, there was no one to blame, but many people who needed forgiving, most importantly, himself.

Paul had been born with a cleft palate. For reasons unknown to him, his parents had chosen not to have this problem corrected until he was sixteen years old. After his earliest years were spent in a some-what closed and highly supportive community, his family moved when he was thirteen to a larger, more diverse city. He recalled his earliest days there and the humiliation he felt when he was teased by his peers and especially by the girls he was only beginning to notice with the eyes of a pubescent boy. A bright and studious boy, he said that he retreated to his studies and spent all of his high school years "in a book or a lab." All that study served him well, and he went on to college and graduate school and eventually dated a few girls after college until he met Diane, fell in love, and they married. A shy and compassionate woman, she was his only sexual partner.

He learned also that just beneath the surface, he was filled with anger and hurt and shame from his adolescent period. He did in fact blame his parents for not taking action to correct his disfigurement sooner, and he was furious with them, despite a superficial cordial relationship. He seldom visited them or welcomed visits from them and kept conversations to reports on the children's progress and his parents' health. He regarded his former classmates with disdain. One day, talking about a bullying event that occurred in the gym at the new school, he heard himself say to me, "But I hear he's a drug addict now and doing time in jail. He was a loser even back then," and when he heard that, he looked at me and sighed. "I sounded like I was fif-teen years old when I said that." I said, "Yes, because you were; that was the wounded boy talking, and he's probably got a lot more he needs to say before you can move on."

In order to heal, it is necessary to visit the past, not to find whom to blame or to linger in the sense of injury, but to uncover and discover all that must be redeemed in order to live our best lives in the present. It starts with remembering and reviewing the events and people through the lens of the present, a lens that has been sharpened and clarified through life experience and softened with love. The journey backward should only be made when love is present. This love can be a renewed compassion for self naturally emerging in the course of a life, or it can be love carried by a companion, a therapist, a friend, or other support person, but to make the journey without love is to risk re-injury.

In the presence of love and carried by the individual commitment to honesty, everything, absolutely everything, can and must be forgiven and, in forgiveness, redeemed. Everything we leave in the past haunts us to some degree, but blessed by redemption, the past becomes the foundation for a better future.

Paul finally admitted that when he first came in, he actually hadn't asked his sweet Diane for the gift of her affection. So profound was his fear of rejection, he had either said nothing or hinted ever so obliquely that he was lonely for her love. Given her reserved nature, the very nature he had chosen her for, she had kept her own needs quiet as well. As Paul became able to risk and the two of them began to speak more openly about their needs and wishes, the old affection returned, as Paul described it to me, "with something added—more warmth."

Paul was a successful person, living a life of integrity and achievement. A good man with a flawless track record, he had every reason to hope for a bright future. Yet he carried within him wounds that had formed psychic scar tissue of resentment and avoidance. He correctly understood that in the present, the wounds themselves were not his problem—they were in the past. But the scar tissue was very much in the present and formed a barrier to love. Thus it is with all of us. The wounds of the past have their effect in the present through the ways we learned to adapt to them or to protect ourselves from further injury. We can never remake the past, but we can remake the effects of the past, by remembering, reclaiming what was lost, reevaluating in light of new understanding, and most significantly, redeeming all through the power of forgiveness. The past is never past, but we have the power to make it new.

The present was an egg laid by the past that had the future in its shell.

—Zora Neale Hurston, African-American author

HELP

Having learned and accepted that it's all up to you, that only you with profound honesty and self-discipline can build a life worth living, you next discover to your consternation that you can't do it alone. No one can. We aren't made to be separate from others. Granted, there are individual differences in our need for and tolerance of other people, but few are meant to live in solitude, and we all need teachers, guides, companions, and the occasional rescuer. That seems to be universal, a fundamental aspect of this being human. People live in groups and long to belong and go to great lengths to find their tribe or to fit in where they are. We need each other for many things, not least of which is to help us on our journey to self.

The tricky part is this: not all help is helpful. One of the tasks of becoming is to learn to sort through the offerings and discover how to separate the wheat from the chaff, in other words, to make clear and fine discriminations about what helps and what hinders.

At first, this appears an impossible task. We make mistakes and take detours that lead nowhere or to dangerous territory. We confuse abdication (ours) with assistance (theirs): we accept control to avoid responsibility. We let ourselves be led by false prophets and gurus and then wonder how we got to this place. Disappointed, disillusioned, we may fall back on an illusory self-reliance—I can do it on my own—or quickly find another savior, quick fix, or fantasy solution.

This mistaking misuse for aid, too, seems to be universal, or if not, so common that billion-dollar industries are made from people's search for solutions. And it happens daily everywhere in the private domain as well. A man promises love and demands control. A woman offers care and delivers dependency. A family takes in an abandoned child for the income he or she brings. A friend breaks a confidence. A lover betrays. A parent criticizes; a spouse withholds.

Make no mistake. A false promise is misuse, often abuse. It's wrong to say that this or that product or program will cure what ails you when you know that it won't. It's wrong to say, "I love you," when what you feel is desire or loneliness and you are willing to lie to take care of that need. There's nothing wrong with desire or loneliness, but manipulating others to serve them does harm.

Where, then, can we find the help we need, and how can we know what to look for? What helps and what hinders? What kinds of things do we need help with? Where do we go to look for that help? How can we recognize it when it comes?

Sometimes we need help with the practical business of survival and enduring. Our journeys may take us into poverty, homelessness, injury, or illness. Then we need help. Oh, we must do our own part—no circumstance relieves us of our responsibility to care for and provide for ourselves—but we will need help, too. It's here that we will need to call on our deepest reserves of humility and reach out and ask and keep asking until we find what we need. Even here, our responsibility is to identify what the need is and whether the help that is offered will in fact help. If I am hungry, I need to be fed, but even more I need help in learning how to feed myself or to break down the barriers that keep me unfed. If I am ill, I need to be treated with procedures and medicines, but I also need to learn how to care for myself, and I may need help in persevering with that. If I am homeless, I need shelter, and I also need help in untangling the web that led to my homelessness and encouragement to stay the course. In none of these cases do I need for you to fix me or my life. I need the helpers to play their part as well as they can, and I need to be treated with respect and dignity and care. The rest is up to me.

These principles hold for the psychological and spiritual journey as well. When I am unfed, unhomed, unwell, or unloved, the responsibility is mine, but I will need help. And it's up to me to find that help and choose wisely. I will need to discover what needs care and attention and where to find what I need. I must not allow myself to be abused in the process, or if I am, I must find a way to heal from that and continue on. There is no other way. I can't give up on myself no matter who else has nor let myself down even if others have in the past.

A young man called Dylan contacted my office one day and said that he needed to "see someone" about his problem with addictions to alcohol and drugs. He said that he had completed three months of intensive treatment and wanted to continue his work with a therapist who was knowledgeable about chemical dependency. The office manager scheduled an evaluation appointment for the following week and provided me with the basic information she had collected from him and from the medical records of the treatment facility. Reviewing this, I could see that Dylan's addiction to alcohol and several drugs had indeed progressed to the severe stage even though he was only thirty-one years old. His history included problems with employment, education, family relations, and law enforcement. The treatment team at the facility he attended stated in his discharge summary that he had made excellent progress after a rocky start, including three episodes of relapse, one of which was nearly fatal. At the time of our appointment, he had been abstinent for sixty days and was now living on his own and employed at his family's business as a sales representative. His aftercare plan called for attendance at AA or NA daily, weekly individual therapy sessions, and weekly aftercare therapy groups at the facility.

I liked him immediately. A tall, athletic man, he was soft-spoken and well-mannered, with an easy smile that reached his eyes. The history he provided matched up with the information I had received from the professionals, and he seemed to have a good understanding that addiction is in fact a disease process and that his own had reached dangerous levels. He assured me that he was more than willing to work hard to maintain his hard-won sobriety and that he understood that anything less than total commitment to that cause would leave him vulnerable to a return of the active disease.

And we began. The therapist's role in this stage of the addiction treatment process lies primarily in helping the client uncover those inner conflicts and pressures that may have contributed to the onset of alcohol and drug abuse and that surely would compromise attempts to stay sober if left unresolved, and then to help the client learn new ways of understanding and dealing with painful memories or emotions. We often talk about the past and its effects on the present, not to find blame or even causes, but rather to encourage understanding and acceptance and to uncover hidden reserves.

Dylan told me that he drank because he liked it and because his friends did, and that naturally led to drug use, and both increased over time in what seemed to him to be an inevitable, even organic, sort of process. He understood that something in his genetic makeup predisposed him to become addicted and that now that he was abstinent, he was sure that he would stay sober with regular attendance at meetings and the accountability that entailed.

In other words, he said, "I don't have any emotional problems or traumatic stuff in my background. I had a happy childhood. I just have the gene." Before I met Dylan, I had worked with literally hundreds of people with addiction problems, so his words came as no surprise to me. I understood that he was at the beginning of a journey that would require much more of him than he currently had any knowledge of. One of the things I knew that he didn't was that he would have to learn to ask for help. I didn't know why or how he had grown into someone who didn't know that he needed help, but he had, and we would need to find a way together for that understanding to emerge safely without harm to him. And then we would need to build a foundation of trust so that when he needed help, he would be able to find it.

Slowly, slowly, we walked back through his life, which had in fact been relatively free of the major traumas and gross mistreatments that many people experience. He was healthy, intelligent, from an intact family who loved and supported one another in most ways, and though generally a quiet man, he was not awkward or unusually shy. His parents were affluent business owners who personified the "self-made" story. High school graduates, they had started a small business, worked long, hard hours, made wise decisions, stayed free of debt and dissolution, and grew their business into a highly successful company. Dylan was the third of four children, who all worked in the family business with one exception, a sister who had become an attorney and lived in another state. Dylan was the only family member with an active and known addiction problem, but he thought that his paternal grandfather might have been alcoholic from the stories he'd heard about his drinking and about his temper.

I listened. I asked questions about this and that. I didn't argue with his notion that emotions or inner conflicts played no part in his addiction story. The truth is, I couldn't say for sure that they did. That's usually the case, but each person is unique, and each person is the expert on himself or herself. While I knew a lot more about the disease of addiction, its contributing factors, and the usual course of the recovery process than he did, he knew a lot more about himself than I did. So I listened.

At our third or fourth session, he came in, and he said, "I almost blew it last night, and I really need to get this off my chest." And that's all it took. He told me about an argument with his father over a work issue that left him feeling helpless and angry and frustrated and said that he didn't know what to do when he felt that way and had seriously considered drinking his feelings away. And then he said, "Oh, that's what you meant. Well, yeah, I guess anger has always played a part in my drinking, especially anger at my dad. I don't know how to change that."

And so we began. With those words, Dylan asked for help, and when he did that, he opened the door to his new life. The life he would get to have when he learned that it was never all up to him and that there were people who wanted to help and could help.

We worked together for about a year, and he stayed sober and I had the privilege of being there for that. Dylan's commitment to his recovery inspired me and reminded me that we are all more alike than different, despite our precious individuality. How we want to be self-sufficient and fear being vulnerable by exposing our weakness and pain. And yet, when we grow brave enough to do just that, when we open ourselves to another and admit we need help, we are softened and strengthened by it. Our need becomes our ally on our return to wholeness.

We all need help sometimes. It may take courage and discernment and persistence to find the help we need, but it is imperative that we keep moving toward it. No one does it all by themselves. We aren't made that way. Don't even bother to try.

Humility is the solid foundation of all virtues.

—Confucius, Chinese philosopher, circa 500 BC

18

STORYTELLING

The more personal you are willing to be and the more intimate you are willing to be about the details of your own life, the more universal you are.

—Sherwin B. Nuland, American surgeon and university professor

In 1979 Lenore Walker published her groundbreaking book titled *The Battered Woman*. With that book, she introduced the world to a tragic, yet common, story that had previously gone untold. Telling that story opened the door to change.

Domestic violence was of course not a new phenomenon in 1979. What was new was that someone—Walker—found a way to tell the story so that large numbers of people could hear. Perhaps it also needed to wait until the social and political climate was open to hearing. In any event, the story, once told, created change in society and in individual people's lives.

Thousands of women suddenly heard their own deeply personal and shamefully secret story told out loud and knew for the first time that they were not alone. With that knowledge came power, the power to ask for help or to move away from or against the conditions that previously seemed insurmountable.

That's the power of story. The right story at the right time produces change.

Not too long after the publication of that book, I attended a conference at which Dr. Walker gave a presentation on her research and described her newly named syndrome. I was there to acquire continuing education hours and because I had agreed to serve on a committee to establish a battered women's shelter in our city. As she talked and I listened, I began to understand that she was describing me, that I personally had been a participant in this story. I honestly hadn't known it until then. The part of my life that followed that particular story line had ended nearly ten years earlier when I divorced my first husband and started the long journey to building a new life.

I could have told you many things about why my marriage failed and likely I had some negative things to say about my former husband, but none of them would have included the patterns of control and domination that Dr. Walker was now describing and I was hearing for the first time. Nor had I any previous knowledge of the phenomenon she described as learned helplessness, which perfectly described my sense of powerlessness and futility during that time.

I literally trembled in my chair in that huge auditorium. Tears started to flow, and a voice in my head (or maybe my heart) said, "That's me—she's talking about me. I was a battered woman. Now I understand."

I confess that among my first reactions was fury at my former husband, still present in my life as the father and co-parent of our children. I'm not sure why, but from someplace I found the restraint not to confront him with this new information. He would need to come to his own understanding in his own time, and it was not my job to educate him or punish him. I did find another woman to talk to, and that helped me integrate this new narrative into my understanding of my experience. Eventually I carried it into therapy and found even broader and deeper clarity. At some level, that's what therapy is and always has been—the process of telling and then reinterpreting one's own unique life story.

Over time, as I worked with this new information, I came to see both of us, my husband and myself, as simultaneously victims and survivors of the drama we enacted with each other. He was not a monster, nor was I either completely without blame or entirely at fault. We both played our parts with the knowledge and ability we had at the time, and we both made mistakes. It was sad, but fortunately not tragic, and we both had the possibility of making different choices in the future. I determined to try, and knew that I would need to do lots of work on understanding myself—my needs and motivations—to avoid re-creating that same dynamic in future relationships.

The power to change and the potential to forgive were the gifts of the story. Only when I could see my story as part of the bigger story, the human story, could I redeem it. Only with the grace of knowing that I was not alone could I begin to share and heal my shame. Only with the help of the larger story was the observer self within me activated so that I could see without judgment and claim without blame. I could accept that the facts would stand, but their meaning was open to interpretation and could be used for good or ill. That would be up to me. I could tell this story however I chose, but how I chose to tell it would have consequences for the person I would become.

I've often wondered what led me to be in that place at that time. Was it merely coincidence, as some would have it? Or was I guided there by my own inner wisdom or by a healing hand? Can we know the answer to that question? Perhaps not, but here's what I believe. When we set out with the best intention we can muster to try to make the most of ourselves that we can, the universe and whatever guides it conspire with our own unconscious wisdom to create precisely the opportunities we need to move forward. I call it grace. It seems to be working all the time. My job is to keep showing up and paying attention, and to receive it gratefully.

They both (two patients) took heart from a myth that mirrored their situation, provided them with insight into the way they reacted to new demands, and gave a larger meaning to their struggle.

—Erich Neumann, German psychologist and author

19

CHANGING, BECOMING

Each one of us has to find the particular feminine
archetype that makes our life meaningful.
—Marion Woodman, Canadian author and Jungian analyst

orraine's first visit to my consultation room was in response, or rather reaction, to her daughter's life-threatening relapse with the drugs that had nearly cost her everything in the past. Lorraine had decided the day before that she could no longer try to handle the stampede of emotions that had trampled her since she got the news a month earlier. "I grabbed my handbag and drove directly here. I knew I had to do something." Our administrator had talked with her and found a way to accommodate her in my schedule for the following day.

We began. She told me of her daughter's troubles and all the ways she had tried to help over the nearly thirty years of adolescent rebellion, drug addiction, and failure to thrive even after the daughter, Karin, achieved abstinence at age thirty-five. Now forty-two, Karin had resumed using drugs when her marriage ended and she was unable to move on emotionally. In the midst of this session, Karin called. When Lorraine saw the number on her mobile, her compulsion to answer was visible. And she did. A few seconds into the call, I saw her begin to relax as she realized her daughter was for the moment reasonably stable. She said, "Maybe that's a good thing. I could see myself through your eyes, and I saw how out of control I am. Oh, and by the way, I hate retirement! I am invisible."

Approaching seventy, Lorraine had been retired for two years from a highly successful business career. She was a self-made woman who grew up in a working-class family and managed to educate herself and achieve more than she ever imagined possible. As the primary, and often sole, wage earner in her family, she worked hard and long and succeeded all along the way. She spoke of the pleasure she took from her work and from the respect of peers, employees, and the young people she mentored. Now, she said, she felt like a failure. She believed she had failed her daughter, and her current life felt empty and meaningless.

Adjustment to retirement is often challenging for women as well as men. People who have achieved a great deal often suffer the most. Lorraine had invested much in her career and had received much in return. In her role as professional, she was valuable and valued. Now that was gone, and nothing had replaced it.

Similarly, the role of mother was comfortable and compelling to her. She took on her daughter's problems as hers to solve, as her mission and as her reason for living. She found purpose and pleasure in helping her. For a time, that worked. She had helped her go to college and find work and had served as her daughter's primary confidant and emotional support throughout her period of abstinence. Now she again cried out to be saved, but this time Lorraine was out of ideas for how to do that. She had tried everything she knew, and her beloved child was still lost.

And so was she. The two roles that had sustained her for her adult life were both gone. Realizing that Karin was forty-two years old and would have to save herself and that the old structures of her professional life were also gone, Lorraine felt lost, frightened, and angry.

So I told her about the triple goddess. The triple goddess refers to the imagery of the feminine archetype characterized by three aspects loosely correlating to the life span of a woman—virgin (maiden)/mother (mature woman)/crone (old woman)—and to the notion that each actual woman carries all three potentials throughout her lifetime, but may express one more strongly than another at a certain time or over time. Each aspect has her unique qualities and attributes, and these roughly correspond to the functions or roles she is expected to perform. So the virgin is youthful, adventurous, and enthusiastic, but also innocent, modest, and timid at times. The mother's primary function is generative and caregiving, whether that is realized by giving birth or by caring for others in the public or private spheres. The crone is the gatekeeper to the other worlds, both death and mystery. She carries some of the energy of the mother and the virgin, but has also the wisdom gained from experience and from her closeness to the hidden secrets of the universe.

Lorraine had only known her mother aspect. Drawing on the strengths of the mother archetype, she had made strong affiliations with her daughter, her husband, and her colleagues. She took good care of all of her responsibilities and drew her identity from her connections and her service on behalf of others. Her virgin qualities had operated beneath the surface at least to the extent that self-determination and activity in the outer world are virgin qualities. She perhaps missed some of the playful gifts of the virgin, but she saw herself as "spunky" and assertive, both good virgin attributes. The part of herself she needed now and did not know at all was the crone.

Funny how this works. The next time I saw Lorraine, she had found a support group of women to help her make better decisions about her actions in relation to her daughter, and she had accepted my suggestion that she start to journal, writing about her fears and feelings of loss and despair, but also her hopes and dreams. She had let her daughter's calls go to voice mail once or twice and had limited herself to one call a day to check on her. Not long after, she found a volunteer job working at a nature center, a big step away from the corporate life she had left, but she was excited for the opportunity to try something new and make a positive contribution. She began to talk of her fear of death and the way that aging brought that into focus.

Her crone was emerging, summoned by the necessity of grief and the surrender to the inevitability of failure. The virgin and the mother can contain neither. Their functions are generative and creative. Only the crone has the wisdom and the spaciousness needed to hold our losses and find meaningfulness within them. That's why we think of her as witch or hag—she holds everything we want to deny or at least postpone.

If she stays the course, Lorraine will travel next to the intersection where virgin, mother, and crone come together. Where wisdom, love, and creativity merge into possibility and promise. Some may think it strange that I evoke the word "possibility" in a discussion of the crone, the archetype of the older woman. After all, time is short. How much can be possible? The answer of course is everything. Everything is possible. It only seems impossible to those who count life in years and decades. But life is lived in moments, this one right now. And in it, everything is possible.

Whatever has crowded out growth needs to be recognized and removed.

—Jean Shinoda Bolen, American psychiatrist, author, and activist

20

FEELINGS

The Guest House
This being human is a guest house.
Every morning a new arrival.
A joy, a depression, a meanness,
some momentary awareness comes
as an unexpected visitor.
Welcome and entertain them all!
Even if they're a crowd of sorrows,
who violently sweep your house
empty of its furniture,
still, treat each guest honorably.
He may be clearing you out
for some new delight.
The dark thought, the shame, the malice,
meet them at the door laughing,
and invite them in.
Be grateful for whoever comes,
because each has been sent
as a guide from beyond.
—Rumi, thirteenth-century Persian poet, Islamic scholar, and Sufi mystic

I recently had a call from my client Angela, who said, "I feel terrible. I am angry and sad, and ashamed for feeling like this when I have so much to be grateful for." This was not the first time I'd heard a thing like this. I wager every client I've ever worked with, most of my close friends, and a few casual acquaintances have said something similar. In our culture in this century, we don't care much for "bad" feelings. Indeed, I'm not sure we are much fonder of "good" feelings.

You've probably had someone say to you something like, "It's just a feeling," or "Feelings aren't facts," or "Don't let your feelings get in the way of your good sense." We are taught that we must learn to manage our emotions to get ahead in life. There's truth in these admonitions for sure, but not the whole truth. The rest of the truth is that we need our feelings as much as we need our judgment, our rational thinking processes. We don't really need to learn to control them or dismiss them or suppress them, as we are often taught by experts and by our parents. What we need is to learn to be in right relation to them.

Feelings are guideposts. They are signs and symptoms that we can learn from in the moment and for the sweep of our life trajectory. Feelings are the sign that you are alive and participating in the flow of experience. To cut off feelings is to cut yourself off from life and from others. To suppress feeling is to deny yourself the full experience of being human. To discount your feelings is to discount your truth and the wisdom of your body and your spirit. To deny your feelings is to be dishonest. To ignore your feelings is to shut yourself off from primary self-awareness, and to judge them harshly is to shut down your vitality and your vision.

To be alive is to feel, and what we do with that is the making of us. Feelings are natural responses to stimuli, as natural as breathing or smiling or a bellyache when you've eaten something spoiled. They flow, they change, they flutter in the wind of experience. To begin, we must only notice. Pay attention to each feeling as it appears and then watch how it moves and notice the next feeling that comes along. When strong emotion comes along, notice it too—how it affects your body, your mind, your intention. Try not to judge. Instead, listen and try to understand. What is the message here? Is there something I need to do or not? What is my responsibility?

There is little doubt that feelings can lead to harm. Please note that I do not say feelings cause harm—they don't. People can allow feelings to move them in harmful ways, but that is a failure of attention or a failure of responsibility, not the inevitable result of a feeling.

If I am angry and I strike out, it is because I either failed to recognize the feeling for what it is and let it control me, or because I chose to act on it. I have choices, and the choices I make constitute the shape of my life. It is true that feelings motivate both thought and action, but it is never true that I have no choice in the matter. Day by day, my task is to know myself and to learn from my feelings, and to thus empower myself to make wiser, kinder choices for myself and for how I treat others. To remain unconscious of the flow of feelings within me is to abdicate my responsibility and to choose instead to be controlled by them, to my detriment.

Yesterday, in the course of events, I recall feeling: sad, happy, embarrassed, tender, amazed, annoyed, anxious, excited, and hopeful. This is perfectly normal. Feelings flow as we engage with life. To have feelings or a specific feeling is to be present in the moment. It isn't necessary to act on a specific feeling or to avoid it either. Wait a moment; take the next step, and the feeling will change. That's how they work. Our emotions are a tracking device for our involvement with life. They show us where we are. They map our inner world and guide us toward our proper destination.

What we must do is welcome every one, listen carefully to its message, and claim the gift that's on offer. So when Angela spoke of feeling angry and sad and ashamed, what I heard was that she was engaged with her life, that she was noticing her own experience and trying to make sense of it. Her mistake was to make judgments about that. She seemed to think that she should feel some other way than the way she actually felt.

I, on the other hand, wondered what her feelings were trying to communicate about her condition and what she might learn from that. I wondered how and in what ways she might use that information to grow herself into the woman she could be. So I suggested that she take some time and journal about those feelings and perhaps dialogue with them to understand them better. She resisted the idea; she told me she just wanted to feel better and had called me hoping for reassurance. I said I knew that, but didn't have it to give her. Angela wasn't as broken as she believed she was. She simply needed to learn a new way of relating to her feelings: She needed to make room for them so she could learn from them and be guided by them, as is their proper function.

In the end, she said she would try what I suggested, "but I am not hopeful." I felt sorry to disappoint her and gratified that she trusted me enough to try despite her misgivings and hopeful because I knew that her effort would be rewarded, that the fact of her willingness and her courage would be sufficient. She didn't know yet that her feelings could be her allies, so she was right to be cautious. All she'd been taught so far was that certain feelings were dangerous and should be avoided, that there were correct feelings and incorrect ones. She hadn't learned the poet's lesson that being human is to be a guest house for the emotions, but she will, and as she does, she will come to know that feelings are "guides from beyond," little bits of grace bestowed all day long.

What is more, every one of those potentials rising up in you is valuable, and many need to be expressed in some way. Becoming whole is a game in which you get rid of nothing; you cannot do without these diverse energies any more than you can do without one of the physical organs that make up your body. You need to draw upon everything that is available to you.

—Robert A. Johnson and Jerry Ruhl, American authors and Jungian teachers

21

LETTING GO OF THE PAST

How does one know if she has forgiven? You tend to feel sorrow over the circumstance instead of rage; you tend to feel sorry for the person rather than angry with him. You tend to have nothing left to say about it all.

—Clarissa Pinkola Estes, American author and folklorist

Halloween, the holiday we now celebrate with witches, superheroes, candy corn, and trick-or-treating, was once a somber pagan ritual that marked the end of the harvest and the beginning of winter. The ancients believed that the transition between seasons formed a bridge between the world of the living and the world of the dead and that the spirits of the departed might be seen on these nights. Ancestor spirits were welcomed because they carried wisdom and the legacies of the ages, but some spirits, called ghosts, were thought to be the essences of people who were seeking revenge or who had been confined to earth because of their own wrongdoing while they still lived. Whatever the reason, ghosts were trapped in the mists of the past and forever blocked from moving forward into their own next life.

So, too, for us when we allow ourselves to be haunted by the past, by the ghosts of our failures, our mistakes, our losses, and our injuries. Just as the ghosts remain bound to whatever place or person they were painfully associated with in life, we lock ourselves to the past with resentment and regret. We are literally haunted by our memories so that we can't move forward into our own best lives.

Perhaps Halloween could be more than simply a fun and colorful celebration, as delicious as that can be. Perhaps we could decide to use this holiday as a reminder to turn for a moment away from the light and take a look into the darkness to see what might be lurking there, shadowing our days and stealing our joy. Is there a memory that causes you to flinch or shudder every time it appears? Is there a lost love you still long for? Does an old injury still cause pain? What do you need to forgive yourself for? What do you tell yourself is unforgiveable from your past?

Oddly enough, everything—absolutely everything—can and must be forgiven. Forgiveness does not mean condoning either your own wrongdoing or that of others. Rather, it means that we have decided to accept the fallibility that is part of being human and that we have made the brave and glorious choice to let go and move on. Without forgiveness, this painful thing from the past remains in the present, holding us hostage and blocking our way. It shapes our interactions with others, our participation in the world, and our relationship to self.

So, how does one forgive? The first step is simply to stop running from it. When we've done wrong or had wrongs done to us, we often choose to make excuses or alibis or simply to pretend that the wrong didn't happen. It's easier than it might seem. Of course, it doesn't actually work. As soon as you let your guard down, and you will, you must, it pops back up. Or it creeps into everyday life from your unconscious, appearing as an angry or depressed mood or baffling outbursts or any of a wide variety of numbing behaviors, like food or alcohol or random sex. At some point, to heal, you must stop the running and acknowledge the injury. *Yes, I did that, and these people were hurt and I was wrong. Yes, the action of this other person hurt me, and I have been wounded in this way and it has affected me in all these ways. This is true.*

When we do that, when we face the truth, there is often pain. It feels bad to know we have harmed others or to take a close look at our own wounds. These feelings—shame, betrayal, abandonment, remorse, anger, and injured pride—are hard to bear, but bear them we must to make peace with the past. If we don't feel all the feelings all the way through, forgiveness will be partial or temporary. We don't have to do this alone. We can find someone to talk to—a priest, a therapist, a trusted friend, someone who listens well and doesn't judge—and talk it through. The cure for all problems begins with telling the story.

You will need one bit of information that you may not have known. It's simply this: everyone makes mistakes, everyone does wrong, to be human is to be fallible and sometimes unkind. To be human is to fail. If you have erred or been the recipient of someone else's failing, it merely proves that you are as human as the rest of us and can freely join the human race. We are all of us, all the time, in need of forgiveness and, whether we acknowledge it or not, hoping for grace. If you did wrong, if you failed, you were probably doing the best you knew how at the time, and if not, if you did in fact know better, then you were carrying other needs that were so forceful they overshadowed your judgment or your values. Learn from this. What still needs learning? What needs still go unheeded and press for satisfaction? What will you do now about that?

Other people, too, do the best they can, given their histories and current circumstances. No one of us escapes the forces of culture and society and personal experience. Wrongs done often seemed a correct course from a certain perspective in a certain time and place. Then, too, everyone else, not just you, walks around with a set of unmet needs that sometimes drive their behavior. You may as well forgive them all, for if you don't, you will never be able to forgive yourself.

If what haunts you is an unfulfilled dream or a lost love, rather than hurtful memories, this could be the time that you stop and reflect and grieve, if need be. Learn the lessons the dream taught; discover the aspect of self trapped in the memory, the longing. We don't get desires that can't be fulfilled; we just misinterpret them, concretize them. It wasn't the boy you wanted, it was . . . what? The dream of travel that he represented? A solution for your loneliness? It wasn't the specific job . . . it was what? A firmer hold on financial stability?

The fulfillment of a desire to be of service or to be respected? Great. Where can you get it now? The longing remains precisely because the essence of the dream is right and true for you. The job now is to find a good and true expression for it.

This process may take time and will certainly require a firm commitment to truth and to the extraordinary notion that self-acceptance is the only reliable foundation from which to build a life. You simply must start where you are and go from there.

As for me, I love Halloween. I love the costumes, the little shiver of mystery in the air, and the candy corn. I think this year I'll replay my childhood favorite and dress as a gypsy fortune-teller just for fun. But I think I will also follow my own advice and check in with the darkness, just in case any ghosts are lingering there that need to be released into their futures so that I can find mine.

We cannot change anything until we accept it. Condemnation does not liberate, it oppresses.

—Carl Jung, Swiss psychiatrist and founder of analytic psychology

22

ASSUMPTIONS

The stupidest thing a person can ever do is to believe he's absolutely right.

—Mark Dean, quite possibly the world's best husband

A few years ago, a family moved into our neighborhood toward the end of November, and by the time the movers had finished the unpacking, the house was covered with blue lights. They twinkled from the rooftop, on the eaves, around doors and windows, and in the trees. Now, we live in a neighborhood that doesn't go in much for outside decorations at the holidays. There are only a few houses with lights, and all of these are discreet and white. It's so consistent we thought there might be a building code that regulated it.

But apparently not, since the blue lights remained, and the second year came back up again. Mark and I had begun speculating about the meaning of the blue lights when we first saw them, and we began again when they returned. We thought he might be Jewish and celebrating Hanukkah in some raffish way. We thought he might just like blue—one of our friends said he liked blue and always wanted blue lights but his wife said no.

So finally, Mark was out walking, and the neighbor happened to be in his yard; and Mark decided he would just ask him about the lights. "So, why do you have all the blue lights?" And the neighbor answered, "My wife likes Elvis." Mark must have had a blank look on his face because the man followed with, "So I always give her a blue Christmas."

Never in a million years would we have come up with that answer. None of our speculation came even close. We laughed together at ourselves and affirmed to ourselves that it truly is pointless to try to figure out what people are thinking or what their reasons are. If you want to know, you have to ask them.

It happened that on the very morning that my husband solved the mystery of the blue lights, one of my clients was in my office working hard to try to guess what her lover was thinking. Her behavior had changed, had grown more distant, and my client didn't know what to attribute it to. She was feeling confused and lonely in a relationship that had previously been warm and familiar, if always somewhat emotionally reserved. She offered up at least five possible theories about the change she'd observed. After a while, I said, "Did you ask her?" She said she had asked, but that her lover brushed off her question with, "I don't know what you are talking about. I haven't changed." I said that we can never really know what someone else is thinking or what their reasons are unless they tell us. And then I told her about blue Christmas.

She laughed when she heard the story, and she said, "Oh, that's great, and I'll be able to remember it because of the imagery. I can see his blue lights, and I can see Elvis. So maybe next time I exhaust myself trying to figure someone out, I'll see those blue lights and stop working so hard." We agreed, she and I, that it was no accident that my husband discovered the secret of the blue lights on that particular day. She needed that simple, silly story. The mystery she was trying to solve was in every way so much more significant and, if solved, seemed to her to hold the potential for great pain.

Her need to know the answer to why her partner had changed was real and powerful, and yet, the reality was she couldn't know unless her partner chose to tell her. She could only ask, listen carefully to the response, and then decide with whatever information she actually did have—her own perceptions, her own feelings, and her own instincts—what it meant for her. No amount of speculation would unearth the partner's point of view, nor would it resolve her anxiety. What she could do was own her anxiety, trust her instincts, and make choices based on her own values, perceptions, and beliefs. She decided to wait. And while waiting, to be kind to herself and act with integrity in the relationship.

She understood that in the end and all along, we each are responsible for ourselves and only for ourselves. She hoped that her partner would begin to trust her enough to talk with her more openly about their relationship, but she also knew that she couldn't force that or will that to happen. She also knew that the relationship was important to her and that, because it was, she was willing to wait and hope and be present. If she couldn't know what her partner was thinking, then she would live with that until she could not any longer. Not because she didn't have a choice, but because she made the choice freely and from love.

She didn't fall into the trap of making assumptions as we so often do. We decide on our own what someone else's behavior means, and we act as if that were true. When we do that, we risk taking steps that will damage the relationship or do real harm to ourselves or someone else. Or perhaps the damage we do is entirely internal, in our beliefs, our trust, or our self-image. Or maybe we never decide, but spend our time and our energy working on the answer to the riddle when we could have been working on making our lives or ourselves better. Or just reading a book.

Mark and I often laugh about the blue lights and what they taught us. It really is a waste of time to make assumptions about things you know nothing about, which is almost everything except what you yourself are doing, thinking, and feeling.

Just ask. And maybe, like what happened for us, your answer will be a lovely surprise, like someone giving his wife a blue Christmas because she loves Elvis. And maybe, like my client, you won't get a straight answer, which is an answer in itself, and you'll know more about where to go next. But never, ever, assume you are right about things you know nothing about, like someone else's heart and soul.

Don't make assumptions. Find the courage to ask questions and to express what you really want. Communicate with others as clearly as you can to avoid misunderstandings, sadness and drama. With just this one agreement, you can completely transform your life.

—Don Miguel Ruiz, Mexican author and teacher of Toltec spirituality

23

DRUDGE DIARY

Before enlightenment, chop wood, carry water.
After enlightenment, chop wood, carry water.

— Ancient Zen saying

One of the stories I tell about myself is that I am a person who is easily bored. I frequently complain that something or another is not interesting. Take golf. A lot of people I know love golf, I mean really love it, but I think it's boring. Ride around on a little cart for hours on end and get out every once in a while and hit a ball with a stick and it either goes where you want it to or, most often, it doesn't, but whichever, you get back in the cart and drive a bit and hit it again with the same results. In between, you chat and look at the lovely grounds and try not to run screaming back to your car and some more interesting activity.

I feel the same way about baseball and essentially all other spectator sports. I sort of like sport shooting and tennis, and I thoroughly enjoy fitness stuff like Pilates and weight training and even yoga, but deliver me from the rest of it, please.

I'm more in my element with mental activities. I like games of all sorts—board games, card games, computer games, trivia, that kind of thing. Even these, I like to play for a couple of hours at most and then on to something else. No, I do not have ADHD, although many have asked the question since it became fashionable and everyone thinks they know about it. I am perfectly able to focus on interesting things, just not boring ones.

Which brings me to chores. Household chores are properly referred to as drudgery. A person who does menial household labor is a drudge. Since one of the synonyms for menial is "boring," you might imagine that I would hate housework. In fact, I don't mind cleaning at all. I'm also a person who loves order; cleanliness is next to godliness in my mind, and so cleaning makes sense to me. Also, I'm a fast cleaner, and that means I can go from disordered and dirty to clean and orderly in no time. I get results! I dig results.

But one household chore was complete and utter drudgery to me . . . emptying the dishwasher. The thing I resented most was that as soon as you empty it, it starts filling again, so you know you'll just have to do it again. Plus, there is nothing interesting about it. You put things away into their proper place—the same places every time—and then you wait to do it again. I tried rearranging the cabinets from time to time, but really there are only a few logical choices, and that got a little nutty pretty quick.

Because I resented this chore so much, I began to also resent the other people who live with me. Why didn't they empty the dishwasher? Who said it was my job? I even said these things to those people once in a while. The response I got was rolled eyes or sad faces. You see, these people know me well, and they know that I hate boredom and that I was emptying the dishwasher by my own choice since I'm the one who is in love with order and cleanliness. The sad faces were what did it, forced me to step back and examine myself. I was not only a drudge; I was also a shrew!

The shrew thing got me, and I thought, *OK, Terri, you really have to do something about this.* Life has finally taught me that when I have a problem, it belongs to me, and thus, the solution is also up to me. I explored my options. I thought I could ask someone else to empty the dishwasher or we could take turns. I thought I could just leave it, and we could pull dishes out as we needed them and let the dirties pile up in the sink. As you can imagine, neither of those ideas really worked for me. I knew without a doubt that no one would empty the dishwasher to my satisfaction, and no way, no how, could I live with dirty dishes in the sink.

So it looks like I'm going to continue the drudgery of emptying the dishwasher, like it or not. That's when I got it. I didn't need to change the chore: I needed to change the "not like it" to "like it." I needed to change my attitude.

I thought about all I had been taught about changing attitudes and wondered how to apply those good principles to this situation. I could examine my thoughts and work on correcting my cognitions. I could examine my self-talk or even explore family-of-origin issues. All good ideas, but what I decided instead was to just chop wood, carry water. On this spiritual journey of mine, no task is unimportant. If it's mine to do, it's mine to own and to use. So now I use this time to reflect on my day and to practice mindfulness or to do nothing for a few minutes. Sometimes I wish it took a little longer.

This may seem a small thing in comparison to the deep work of reclaiming the self and forging a meaningful life, but indeed it is not. Anything that regularly steals the joy from our days must be transformed and made whole. After all, life is lived one ordinary day at a time. That's where we find our redemption and our joy.

When you pay attention to boredom, it gets unbelievably interesting.

—Jon Kabat-Zinn, American professor of medicine and mindfulness teacher

PART III

1-10-04

Our anniversary. 18 years.
What a great day that was.
I'm so blessed to have Mark
in my life. We've had a great
time together, for one thing. But
for another, the main thing, I've
felt loved and backed up...
for the first time. He's so good
to me. I'm so lucky.

Journal Entry, 2004

China, 2004

Florida, 2004

LOVE

Love: strong affection for another arising out of kinship
or personal ties; warm attachment, enthusiasm, or devotion;
unselfish loyal and benevolent concern for the good of another.

—Merriam-Webster Dictionary

Love—how can we ever understand it? It's so central to everything and yet so elusive to explanation. Do we even recognize it when we see it? If so, how can it be that we are so often disappointed? Like most people, I've spent a great portion of my life trying to make sense of it. On the one hand, it seems to take so many forms, and on the other, it has also often seemed false or unreliable. How on earth can a person finally come to terms with love?

Make no mistake. Love is the central issue of life from its beginning to its end. Infants fail to thrive without it, and the elderly tell us that the cruelest aspect of growing old is the loss of love through death and through neglect. We humans need to be loved as surely as we need sustenance and safety. And we need to give love as well. Love animates us: it is the force that moves and shapes us; it's where we find home and how we move out into the world.

I recall a moment with my first therapist in our third or fourth session when he said, and this is pretty much verbatim despite the years that have passed, "By all rights, given your history, you should be much crazier than you are. Someone must have loved you very much. Who was that?" I answered, "Yes, my grandfather," without hesitation. And then I told him that story.

I was born just at the end of World War II. My father was overseas, where he would remain for two more years, having shipped out four months before my birth, first to France and then to the Philippines. My mother was living with her parents. So I lived my first two years in a household with four adults—my mother's sister lived there, too—and no other children. I was well cared for. I think they all loved me in their ways, but the love of my early life was my grandfather. When my father came home and he and Mother found a place of their own, I decided to stay with my grandparents, and they let me. So until his death when I was five, I spent every day with my grandfather.

He and I got up before anyone else, and we had pancakes and Luzianne coffee, mine with a lot of milk, and then we left for our walk with Granddaddy's dog, Booger. It may be faulty memory, but what I recall is that we walked all the way to the town cemetery every day—which as an adult I've learned is three miles from their home, so that's a six-mile walk every day for a three- or four-year–old, which seems unlikely, but that's what I recall. What I know for sure is that I was perfectly happy when I was with Granddaddy. He didn't talk much, and we didn't do anything special; we just walked and were together, and I knew that he was exactly where he wanted to be and that we would do it again the next day.

He died when I was five, and while I understand this sounds dramatic, I was never happy again until many years later, when I finally began to grow up and when I could love and be loved again. The other people who might have loved me and might have taught me how to love and be loved simply weren't able to because they were too trapped in their own suffering: they couldn't help me grow up because they hadn't grown up themselves. The love they gave with the best of intent was always contingent on their mental or physical health (my mother) or their business and social interests (my father). I was given everything, even a pony when I was five and a new convertible when I was sixteen, but in most ways, day in and day out, I was expected to fend for myself and to be competent and content. I faked all that really well until the time when I couldn't anymore, but that was well into adulthood, and it wasn't my parents' fault. I don't blame them for their failures of love, since I too have failed to love well and I know that I wanted to and couldn't, and so I assume it was the same for them. We did the best we could, my parents and I, and we let people down. That seems to be what people do.

It is important that I explore the ways my parents failed at parenting and at loving, not to set blame for my problems, but to learn from that exploration how I might have been misled by them, how my expectations may have been distorted and my vision limited. I need to understand them to begin to understand myself. And if I want to understand love, I need to see how they failed, as well as how they succeeded.

Love, in all its forms, begins with understanding, and from understanding, all manner of love becomes possible. Without it, whatever masquerades as love is bound to disappoint. When we come into adulthood carrying all our parents' mistakes as if they were truth, we are bound to stumble. That, too, seems to be what people do. But we can learn to love and to be loved when we clear the path of as much misinformation as we can and find within ourselves that deepest truth—that we are meant for love. That truth awaits on the path of wholeness for each of us. We must only be steadfast in our commitment to self-honesty and self-responsibility.

Granddaddy loved me very much. I wish I could have had him longer, but it was enough. Love is powerful like that. I believe that most of us had someone like my grandfather, some one person who loved us well and set the foundation for future love. But even when we didn't, we can still learn. It may be human to make mistakes, but it is also human to love. We are made that way. Love is as natural to us as breath and as vital. It is the essential element of wholeness. We are made whole by love—of people, of ideals, of virtues, and of the moments of our lives. All the rest of the work we do, the hard labor of self-discovery and the enduring struggle to accept and own our rightful responsibilities, is worth it only because it makes love possible. And love is worth every bit of it.

The beginning of love is to let those we love be perfectly themselves, the resolution not to twist them to fit our own image.

—Thomas Merton, American author, Trappist monk, and theologian

24

PSYCHOTHERAPY 4
THE HEALER

The therapist can interpret, advise, provide the emotional acceptance and support that nurtures personal growth, and above all, he can listen. I do not mean that he can simply hear the other, but that he will listen actively and purposefully, responding with the instrument of his trade, that is, with the personal vulnerability of his own trembling self. This listening is that which will facilitate the patient's telling of his tale, the telling that can set him free.

—Sheldon B. Kopp, American psychotherapist and author

Five years after my three sessions with Richard, my talkative counselor during graduate school, I once again found myself in a therapist's office. I had made a stunning descent to the bottom of my well of reserves. I had used up all my money, all my energy, all my ideas, and all my faith in myself and in the future. My dream of becoming an academic anthropologist had dissolved as mysteriously as it had arisen. The years of education and effort now seemed wasted, and I was discouraged, alone, and afraid. I was working at a variety of temporary clerical jobs and part-time at a bookstore. I had tried going back to mortgage banking, my unloved and discarded previous career, and while the salary was far superior to the wage I earned with my piecemeal employment, I simply couldn't do it. I didn't enjoy it, and, I think, it felt too much like going backward.

My personal life was likewise a disaster. Divorced and without extended family, my close ties were to my children and to a couple of friends who survived the upheavals I had created in my life. My children, now one teenager and one preteen, were frightened for me and for themselves. They didn't see how this woman who was failing to care for herself would be able to take care of them. They were correct.

I found my way to a vocational counselor, who did some testing and evaluation, told me I should be a museum director (huh?), and then offered to use the funding that would ordinarily provide vocational training to pay for twelve sessions of psychotherapy. He could tell from my track record that no amount of education or training would be helpful until I got my insides sorted out. He gave me a referral to a colleague who, he said, was an excellent therapist with strong ethics and a solid reputation. I went, of course. I didn't have much faith that it would help, but I looked forward to having someone, anyone, to talk to.

Harold was a nice man. I can't say exactly why, but I knew right away that, whether he could help me or not, he would not harm me. He was a few years older than me—a tall, lanky man with dark hair and a warm smile. His manner was soft-spoken, a little tentative, and Southern. I liked that. I'd had enough of too-smart, supremely confident folks from other parts of the country while I pursued my education. It was nice to have the assurance, at least on that count, that I would not be judged and found wanting.

There was plenty of other stuff I could count as failures, though.

We started going through them one by one. I think maybe there's a prize at the bottom of the well that you can't find until you make it there. Only at the bottom did I find the courage to just tell my story, without pretense and without protecting my ego. All the secrets that I had held so close, both from my own fear and shame and from the beliefs I had been given in my early years, simply walked out into Harold's office and took a seat. They said, "Here I am, for better or worse, but I'm here and I'm not going anyplace."

I can't say that I felt any sudden seismic shifts as these stories were told and—astonishing—accepted by Harold. I didn't. There were times when something that had previously been confusing suddenly made some kind of sense. There were times when I could honestly see that I had been unnecessarily hard on myself. There were times when I cried and times when I laughed. There were times when I could see that my failure to be honest with myself was holding me back. There were times when I felt frustrated and even annoyed that the answers to my biggest questions still eluded me.

But gradually, over the first twelve sessions and then the subsequent ones I somehow found the money to pay for, little bits of myself were reclaimed, and disconnections of decades standing were rejoined like atoms combining to make molecules. My emotions, long denied or misaligned, began to serve their proper function, to connect me to my truths and teach me about the world.

What did Harold do to make this possible? He listened. He was patient. He was quiet. Sometimes he read me poems or told me about an author that he had learned from. He offered simple options for me to consider when I stumbled into my most rigid places. And then one day, I said, "Can you guess what profession I'd choose if I could do anything at all?" And he said, "You'd be an epistemologist." And that was the right answer!

There aren't that many people in the world who dream of being an epistemologist, and I had never said that to him. So how did he know? He knew because he had listened and because he trusted his intuition and, most importantly, because he understood me.

And that's the curative agent. That's what everyone needs. To be understood. Without it, you will always struggle to find your wholeness. With it, everything is possible.

If I want to understand an individual human being, I must lay aside all scientific knowledge of the average man and discard all theories in order to adopt a completely new and unprejudiced attitude. I can only approach the task of understanding with a free and open mind, whereas knowledge of man, or insight into human character, presupposes all sorts of knowledge about mankind in general.

—Carl Jung, Swiss psychiatrist and founder of analytic psychology

25

LOVE

Love's true nature remains forever beyond the grasp of all
our faculties. It is far greater than any feeling or emotion and
completely surpasses any act of human kindness. . . .
The realization of love always remains mysterious.

—Gerald May, American psychiatrist, theologian and author

No matter the question, love is the answer. No matter the problem, love is the solution. No matter the illness, love is the cure. In the end and all along, love is the only thing.

When I was a young therapist, I once sought counsel from a mentor about a case that had me baffled. I wanted so badly to help my client, a woman of twenty-two years with severe and frightening symptoms, but I had no idea how to do that. I had tried everything I learned in my training, and she remained stuck in her dangerous behaviors and ways of looking at the world. I felt I was failing to reach her and struggling to find the right words to say to create the possibility for change. This kind man heard me out in his quiet way and then offered, "When I don't know what to do to help a client, I just sit and love them. Sometimes that's enough."

I had so many reactions to that statement. Part of me sighed with relief that he also sometimes felt helpless in the face of people's problems. Part of me thought that sounded way too easy, a cop-out. But a part of me knew that what he said was the truest possible thing that could be said. Love is the force that heals. No matter the skill of the clinician, no matter the power of the technique, without love, there is only emptiness and change occurs only at the most superficial level. With love, all things are possible.

Years later, a brilliant woman named Victoria reminded me of this lesson. She was in her late thirties when she came to me, lonely and desperate for a solution to her problems. She introduced herself and said, "I eat too much, I drink too much, I sleep with too many men, and sometimes I find myself in situations that I'm not sure I can get out of. If something doesn't change, I will die soon. I need help." Highly successful in her academic career, she was recognized as an expert in her field and wealthy from the sale of her award-winning books. She lived in a beautiful home in a lakeside community and commuted to conferences and symposia around the world. To her colleagues and students, she was the epitome of the independent accomplished woman. But she had come to see herself as just a woman no one loved. And in the face of this, nothing else mattered.

I asked her to tell me her story. So she told me about her academic career, from kindergarten to graduate school. After a while, I began to ask questions about her family. "Oh, I just had a normal childhood," she said.

So, do you have any brothers or sisters?

No, just me.

Tell me about your mother.

There's nothing to tell. She was an attorney, a nice woman. She's dead now.

And your father?

Also an attorney. I don't know him well. He lives out West.

How old was your mother when she died?

Oh, forty-three, I think.

That's young. Was she ill?

Well, I guess you could say yes. She killed herself.

Victoria's expression never changed as she relayed these facts. But I noticed that she moved ever so slightly deeper into the cushions of the sofa and that her left hand kept stroking the soft blanket I keep on its arm for chilly days. She never broke eye contact with me, but seemed to challenge me to say something comforting that she could refute. I didn't.

Instead, I just sat there and loved her.

After a few seconds, she looked away, and when she looked back, she said, "Do you think there's any hope for me?" I said, "Of course," and we started on the long journey of reclaiming the child who hoped for love, settled for accomplishment, and showed up regularly to demand that her needs be met, if only in the momentary bliss of escape or in the shadowy aspects of love.

Victoria's journey was long and strenuous. With little experience of love, she didn't know how to recognize it or accept it. When it was offered, she pushed it away or didn't notice. She lacked skill in loving others or herself. Neither of us ever knew what caused her parents' inability or failure of love, but slowly she came to see it as theirs, not something inevitable in her. And in fits and starts, she got better at loving and at being loved.

And then she met a man. And he loved her. And she let him. This man was an ordinary man who happened to be really good at loving. Victoria had worked hard and healed some of her wounds and cracked open her armor so love could creep in. Between them, they created a space where love could take root and grow. Both of them understood that living without love had made her awake to it in a way others might not be, and they also understood in some way that he had an unusual gift for it.

Neither of them was particularly religious, but they used the word "blessed" when they spoke of finding each other. I think they meant that grace had found them.

Love is always the answer, and where love is, grace is also.

What is hell? I maintain that it is the suffering of being unable to love.

—Fyodor Dostoyevsky, Russian novelist

26

LOVE SHOWS

Love is that condition in which the happiness of another person is essential to your own.
—Robert A. Heinlein, American science fiction author

A man I know has Alzheimer's disease and lives in a facility for people with impaired memories. His wife visits him every day. He no longer recalls her name, and some of the time, he is unable to make sentences to communicate with others. But somehow, every day he can make one sentence. Every day, he looks at his wife, and he says, "Will you marry me?" And every day, she says yes.

That's what love looks like.

A week or so ago, I was at home writing, and my husband had some errands to run so I asked if he would stop on the way home and get me a "sweet treat." I have a bad sweet tooth and enjoy a treat with my coffee around four o'clock each day. He said, sure, and I went back to work. I heard him come in at three thirty or so, but I kept on with my work until four. Then I went in the kitchen and saw on the counter the following:

> one slice banana nut bread
> one slice lemon pound cake
> one cinnamon apple muffin
> one donut
> and a single yellow sunflower.

That's what love looks like.

My friend Grant went blind from an eye disease. A strong, independent, successful man, he loved travel, fine dining, and people. A combat veteran with many medals for bravery who survived untold hardships in his war, he had firmly embraced all that was civilized, cultured, and comforting in civilian life. He dressed in the finest clothes, had season tickets to the symphony, the ballet, and the opera, and enjoyed nothing more than a visit to an art gallery or dinner with friends. His blindness compromised all his greatest pleasures. But Grant's bravery hadn't left him after the war, and he was determined to continue to the best of his ability. So he did. And his much younger wife accompanied him and softly described the art, the costumes, the dancer's grace, and gently guided the hand that held the fork to the right place on the plate. None of this was ever mentioned and was barely noticeable to others.

That's what love looks like.

My client David, age twenty-four, brilliant, vibrant, talented, gay and closeted, was terrified to tell his parents about his homosexuality. He loved them and feared their disapproval, feared that he would lose their love. Still, he felt he could no longer go on in secrecy because he had met a man and fallen in love, and he wanted to share the beauty and wonder of that with his mother and father. They lived in another state, and he decided to do that by phone, thinking it would give them time to adjust and process it before he saw them in person. Finally he found the courage to make the call. He hoped his mother would answer, but, no, his father did. With his heart beating wildly, he said, "Dad, I have something to tell you. I'm gay." And his father said, "Of course you are. When are you coming home? We miss you."

That's what love looks like.

Briana was nineteen, in trouble in school, using drugs with her friends, drinking too much, and generally making a mess of her life. Gail, her mother, found a therapist who helped her arrange admission to a treatment facility that could help with the substance abuse as well as Briana's emotional problems. Gail then offered Briana the chance to go to treatment. When Briana refused, Gail told her she would need to move out and find a way to support herself. Then, alone in her room, Gail sobbed herself to sleep.

That's what love looks like.

Daniel is in his early seventies, and he's dying of cancer. With chemotherapy and radiation, his life has been extended from the six months originally predicted to three years, and he's holding his own. He never talks about it. What he talks about is the book he just read or his wife's new project, but mainly he asks about you. When our beloved dog died, he sent us a card, called, and offered these words: "I hope you get a new puppy. To move forward, one must replace love with love."

That's what love looks like.

In our little town, there's a handicapped man, Felix, who makes his living by selling fruit and cookies from the basket on the back of his tricycle. He is well cared for by a mother and family and by his own efforts, despite his limitations. Everybody knows him and everybody loves him. But one day, someone decided that he was in violation of the law and that he would need to have a peddler's license to continue to sell his snacks—but our city doesn't offer such a license. The concerned citizen thought he should be made to stop and filed a complaint with the city commission, which was duly placed on the city agenda and published with the rest of the agenda. On the designated day, the commissioners arrived to find hundreds of people waiting outside and more arriving every minute. Every one of them was there to support Felix.

That's what love looks like.

Briana, who chose to move out rather than go to treatment, thought she could make it on her own, thought her mother had exaggerated the problems and that she could handle things just fine. It didn't take long for her to discover that she was wrong. She was ashamed and prideful and didn't want to admit she was in over her head, but she was also desperate. So she called her mother and said, "I'm in trouble." And her mother said, "Come home."

That's what love looks like.

I walk into a room, and my friend Janice smiles to see me.

That's what love looks like.

My neighbor had a heart attack. People took food to her house every day for weeks.

That's what love looks like.

A family is sitting in a waiting room. They've been told their mother/wife/sister/daughter may not make it, following an auto accident. Some softly cry, some pace, some hold the hands of others, someone comforts a child, they wait, they endure.

That's what love looks like.

Love shows. It's not an idea or an ideal. It's physical, tangible, visible, active, and visceral. Love is an energy, and it has energy. It is specific, particular, and realistic. People can only be loved as they are, not as we wish them to be. Oh, we may have wishes for those we love, but the minute we need them to be different than they are, our love is compromised.

Love can hurt, but it always sustains and enlarges. The moment I agree to love something or someone, I have opened myself to the potential for pain. And yet, I have also opened myself to the only possibility for expansion.

What love doesn't do is diminish, damage, possess, or reduce. Those who claim to love and don't—or can't or don't know how—do great harm. The younger the person who is falsely "loved," the greater the harm. There is nothing more dangerous to the developing self than injury delivered in the promise of love. We are all most vulnerable to those we love and those from whom we have the expectation of love—parents, partners, leaders of certain types, caregivers. When we think someone should love us because we are told they should or because they have promised to, and what they offer instead is abuse, neglect, injury, or demands, the disconnect leaves us searching for understanding. Most of the time, it's less painful to believe that it's our fault, that we are somehow insufficient, than to believe that the beloved doesn't truly love or is impaired in some way. So long as the fault lies within us, there's reason for hope. We can try to change, to be better, to be different, to please. If the fault lies within the other, then we are helpless to change it, so our hope of love is lost. And, oh, how we hope for love.

Belinda and her husband, Beck, had been married for ten years when I first saw them in my office. They said that they had a "good marriage," but needed some help in learning to deal with their eight-year-old son's problems. He had been diagnosed with ADHD, was having problems at school, and was increasingly difficult to deal with at home. Beck said he thought that Belinda wasn't strict enough and the boy took advantage of that. Belinda didn't say much at all. Over the course of six sessions as we studied and practiced parenting skills, I heard Beck tell Belinda she was too timid, too fat, and too lazy, that she was "spoiling" their son and that she needed to be stronger, be more consistent, be more patient, spend more time with their son, spend less time with their son, and oh, by the way, "you need to pay more attention to me, especially in bed." Belinda would occasionally defend her actions, but most of the time, she sat silently and let Beck define the situation.

One day I asked Belinda if she would tell us how she saw the problem. She said, "Well, I know Beck thinks I'm wrong and this is a stupid idea, but I don't think our son has ADHD at all. I think he's depressed and acting out to try to get our attention. The doctor and Beck have both told me I'm wrong, but it's still what I think. I wish we could take him to another doctor."

Beck said, "See, that's just another example of you taking his side and spoiling him. He's not depressed. He's got ADHD, and we are going to have to work together to get him in line." Belinda folded in on herself, sliding back into her usual silence, one hand stroking the other, her sadness tightly bound, but so apparent, I wondered how Beck could possibly not see.

I don't think Beck was a bad man, but I think he didn't love his wife. I think she knew he didn't and was still in that place where she blamed herself and was trying really hard to win his love. I didn't ask that question, and I've often wondered how he would have answered, but I think he would have said, "Of course I love her," and believed that to be true. But the way he was with her is not what love looks like.

People can disagree and argue and still love. People can say unkind words to each other and still love. People can have profound differences about vitally important issues like child-rearing and still love. But love listens, and shows respect, and appreciates, and validates, and waits. Love reaches out rather than pushing away. Love tries to understand and cares when the other is hurting, even when love knows it's the source of the pain.

I don't know what happened to Beck and Belinda. They finished their parenting skills module, and I referred them to a colleague for marital counseling and to another parenting class. I did suggest that Belinda share her thoughts with the child's physician once more. I hope that didn't cause her more pain. My colleague told me they didn't follow up with him, and I wasn't surprised. Few people are willing to try counseling until and unless they genuinely have a desire to make the relationship work—even if it requires personal examination and change.

When I think of them now, I hope that one of them found the courage to speak up and ask for more. Both of them were suffering from the blockage of love. Belinda carried the sadness and Beck carried the anger, but both emotions belonged to both of them and together they kept love away. Love can only thrive where emotions are welcome and treated with kindness and respect as well as restraint. Love can only thrive where people are willing to take responsibility for their choices, their words, and their feelings. Belinda and Beck blamed each other, he in words, she in silence, but neither of them was yet willing to own their part in the problem. Neither was willing to grow up and be accountable for themselves. Love can't live there. Love can only live where two striving-for-wholeness people agree to strive together. Love is a gift, but it must be cherished, and to cherish is to pay attention and handle with care.

It has been said that people love what they care for, and I believe that's true. For love to endure and grow, we must be willing to care day in and day out, in hard times and soft, through laughter and tears, when we ourselves are strong and when we aren't. Love is active; love is concrete; love is real.

You can know it when you see it—you'll say, "This is what love looks like."

Love doesn't just sit there, like a stone, it has to be made, like bread; remade all the time, made new.

—Ursula K. Le Guin, American author

27

LOVE AND MARRIAGE

Never love anyone who treats you like you're ordinary.

—Oscar Wilde, Irish playwright

If it's not unconditional, it's not love. It's something else, and it's almost always destructive. "Love" that demands or exchanges or controls or withdraws isn't love exactly. It's love's facsimile, and it always harms the recipient because it confuses them and makes them feel at fault. Love in all its forms isn't necessarily mutual or shared. Mother Teresa loved the people she helped whether they loved her or not. The Dalai Lama appears to radiate love to all he meets and to feel a genuine love for humanity. But in marriage or other partnered relationships between two people, if it isn't mutual, it probably isn't love. It may be dependency or habit. It may be domination or need. It may even be passion or desire, but none of these are love.

Love is the willingness to see and be seen, to speak and listen, to share, to embrace, to mourn and hang on, to work if work is needed, to rest in what is. If you have to ask if it's real, it isn't. It may be headed there, but it isn't there yet. You will need to become more honest, more open, more vulnerable, and more curious. You will have to let go of expectations and see what is there—you will have to learn who this person, this other, really is. You will have to let down your guard. Then, and only then, can love arrive.

Neither beauty nor wealth nor accomplishment guarantees love. And we can't earn it with good works or sacrifice. Indeed, if any of these are the condition for love, then by definition, it isn't love. Love doesn't demand—it allows, it accepts, it affirms, and it understands. That is, love sees things as they are and knows that inevitably they will change and makes room for that, too. The woman I was when my husband married me no longer exists except as a memory and in the shadows of my soul. My husband has seen me grow and falter and change into other sorts of women over time, and he's loved all of them. He would tell you that my spirit has always been the same, and that might be true, whatever it means, but I know and he acknowledges that I've changed enormously since the day we were wed.

What would have happened if his love didn't have room for that? What would have happened if his love had demanded I remain that woman (who, for the record, was much more accommodating and self-denying than the woman I am now and therefore might be much more attractive to a certain type of person)? I didn't earn his love by being a particular way in terms of appearance or personality or attribute. He took a look at me and decided to give me his love and to do the work required for it to grow. He didn't work on me—he worked on himself, and he worked with me to grow the relationship. That's the work of love. And over any significant period of time, there is no love without that work. Period.

But, oh, my, it sure is worth it. I think there is no greater joy than that of a loving marriage. I was surprised to learn from a Catholic priest that within the church, it is believed that people can be called to the religious life or called to marriage and the family life. I didn't fully understand, until he told me that, why marriage is considered a sacrament. Now I understand. It truly is a holy calling, whether we're Catholic or of some other religion or none at all, because it will accept no less than our best and most diligent effort and urges us onward to our highest selves.

Not all good marriages look alike, but they do have some things in common. I don't presume to know all of them, but I do know some. They are based on respect. They include good manners, laughter, shared values, a talent for forgiveness, and a million tiny decisions to remain committed. Commitment is not, as some might think and it has been described, a once and forever thing. Commitment is done over and over and over again. It flows gently or demands rethinking. It is subject to the humanity of its bearers and to the vagaries of life; it is a discipline that when practiced provides the ground for the flowering of lingering love.

I want to know all I can know about married love, and so I pay attention to the stories that come my way and to the people I know who seem to have it. These stories are my teachers, and I am their eager student. Since life and love didn't come with a set of instructions and I have discovered that I must find my own way, I am thankful to learn from people like these.

My friend Marilyn says she had been married to her husband, Joseph, for forty years, through long careers and career upheavals, four children from birth to adulthood with all the joys, complexities, and sorrows that children bring, many losses, many celebrations, arguments, betrayals, boredom, sex and no sex, austerity and prosperity, success and failure—when she looked at him across the room dressed in his ratty bathrobe with uncombed hair and two days of stubble as he made a mess on the kitchen counter and fell madly, passionately, permanently in love with him. She explains it this way. She said it took all of that for her to get to know him, and you can't really love someone until you know him.

Brenda and Darren met and fell in love at AA. Old-timers in AA advise against the kind of romance they had, Darren with fifteen years of recovery, Brenda with only two, and an age difference of twelve years. Both of them were committed to staying sober, but people thought they were putting their sobriety at risk with the relationship. They ignored the warnings, stayed together, and after a while, married. That was twenty years ago. They say that God gave them each other with only one condition—that they treat the relationship exactly like the gift it is. It seems to be working.

My husband says driving with me as his passenger is like driving with the cops in the car. We both laugh because we both know it's true and because we are both grateful for the honesty we have with each other. Neither of us needs the other to be perfect. His bad driving and my nagging about it are familiar and comfortable to us both, and we both understand that a long love is partially built with a forgiving attitude and lots of laughter.

Phyllis and Frank met in college, married, had careers and children, and now they've grown old. She can no longer see. He combs her hair and makes sure her clothes go together. She grumbles a bit, but picks up her cane and goes to dinner with him.

Patrick is an author and former teacher. He's married to a nurse. He's famous—she's not. They are each other's heroes. He says she's the kindest, most generous and committed woman he's ever met, and a wonderful mother. She says he's brilliant and funny and patient and a terrific father. They tell other people these things, and they tell each other, too.

Kelly and David are thirty-something young professionals who met two years ago. Both had several relationships before this one, and they each say that this is the real deal, that no one else ever came close. They plan to marry next year and start a family right away while biology is on their side. Both sets of parents are still married to their original spouses and have solid relationships. Neither Kelly nor David has any major trauma or illness or impairment to stand in their way. They are smart and beautiful and, I think, morally sound young people. So, maybe, just maybe, if they each work really hard at becoming whole, they will endure, and their love will grow and mature along with them. Wouldn't that be wonderful?

An honorable human relationship—that is, one in which two people have the right to use the word "love"—is a process, delicate, violent, often terrifying to both persons involved, a process of refining the truths they can tell each other.

It is important to do this because it breaks down human self-delusion and isolation.

It is important to do this because in doing so we do justice to our own complexity.

It is important to do this because we can count on so few people to go that hard way with us.

—Adrienne Rich, American poet, author, and feminist

28

HEARTBREAK

> To love at all is to be vulnerable. Love anything and your
> heart will be wrung and possibly broken. If you want to make
> sure of keeping it intact you must give it to no one, not even an
> animal. Wrap it carefully round with hobbies and little luxuries;
> avoid all entanglements. Lock it up safe in the casket or coffin of
> your selfishness. But in that casket, safe, dark, motionless, airless,
> it will change. It will not be broken; it will become unbreakable,
> impenetrable, irredeemable. To love is to be vulnerable.
>
> —C. S. Lewis, English author, academic, and Christian philosopher

To love at all is to be vulnerable. When we love, we are sure to get our hearts broken. Hearts break in many ways and for many reasons, but to love is to risk the certainty of pain at some point down the path. My first major loss was the death of my grandfather when I was five, and soon after, the death of my beloved cocker spaniel, Princess. My parents tried their best to protect me from both losses, sending me to stay with friends when Granddaddy died and keeping the death of Princess secret from me until the little boy next door told me. He had heard it from his parents. Mother told me Princess was at the doctor's office and would be home soon. I think she thought I would forget about her since I was just a child.

Their protection, of course, did more harm than good. One can never say with certainty precisely what an effect from early childhood was, but I recall fury that my parents lied about Princess, and the time I spent with Mother's friends after Granddaddy died is my first memory of feeling "less than." I was watching the mother of that family tie ribbons in her daughter's hair, and I remember thinking, "There must be something wrong with me that nobody wants me at home."

We never talked about Granddaddy's death even though it changed our lives in dramatic ways. Soon after, my parents moved into a new house large enough for all of us and my grandmother closed the home we had lived in with my grandfather. A few months later, my mother became ill for the first time and was never really healthy again. I don't know if there's any connection between Mother's illness and the loss of her father, whom she adored, but there is surely a convergence in time that had meaning for my child self. All I can say with certainty is that before Granddaddy died, I remember happiness, and after, all I remember is fear and sadness.

That's not to say there weren't happy times and fun times and laughter and love in our house. There was plenty of all that, but there was also a shadow, an underlying anxiety that nothing good would last and that somehow none of it was real. I got a new dog, Punchy, a little Boston terrier, who was my constant companion; and when Mother was sick and Daddy was working, Grandmother and Punchy kept me company and kept me safe. But I missed my mother and I missed my Granddaddy, and I didn't know how to talk about it or what to ask for and no one else seemed to either. So I kept it to myself and pretended as well as I could that everything was fine.

I didn't know then what I have since learned: that loss and its pain are universal. I didn't know that others felt the way I felt or that everyone is sometimes in need of comfort. I just concluded that there was something wrong with me and set out to hide my imperfection and try to figure out how to fix it. And that was my story for the next twenty years or more.

When Mother died too young, I was a young mother myself and in a failing marriage, and I tried to handle that loss the way I had learned, by repressing and coping. I didn't grieve. I didn't know how, and there was no one to help. My parents had divorced two years before Mother's death, and Dad had married a woman who was about my age and very possessive of him and defensive with me. I didn't like her, but I pretended to because I loved my father and didn't want to lose him. My husband thought I should just get on with things and take care of him and our child. He had said many hateful things about Mother over the years of our marriage, so there was no warmth for me there. I took it in and walked on. Years later, a part of my healing came from finally grieving the loss of my mother and all the losses that she and I experienced together during her life. Now, when I think of her, I smile.

I wish I had known back then what Alice Walker so eloquently taught in her book *The Way Forward Is with a Broken Heart*. For all of us who love, the way forward is always with a broken heart. To love inevitably leads to heartache. That's the way of things. Resistance is futile, and avoidance is destructive: love is always worth the pain, but the pain is real and needs our compassionate attention. The broken heart can lead us forward; the frozen heart stands still.

I don't overstate when I say that every client who has made his or her way to my consulting room has come because of grief. Sometimes the client is aware of the grief: he has come because of the loss of an important person through death or through separation, estrangement, or abandonment, or she has lost an important activity or life goal. Other times the grief is lurking beneath the surface of things, and the client has come with concerns about mood or behavior. But always the grief is there. To be human is to experience loss, and the natural response to loss is grief. We may need help grieving. That help may be in the form of a listening ear or a gentle touch or a shared remembrance. We each grieve in our own way and our own time. What we can do for ourselves is learn to respect that process, make room for it, and treat ourselves with the gentlest of care while we mourn. Our grief, after all, simply means that we have loved and love still, and love is always the answer.

Nor must we see grief as a step toward something better. No matter how much it hurts—and it may be the greatest pain in life—grief can be an end in itself, a pure expression of love.

—Gerald May, American psychiatrist theologian and author

29

WORK

The secret of happiness is not in doing what one likes,
but in liking what one does.

—J. M. Barrie, Scottish novelist and playwright

On Christmas morning in 1995, I was on a train from Cuzco, Peru, to Machu Picchu. We had been in Cuzco for several days, where our hotel was a former monastery and where the coffee was delivered to my room strong and hot almost before I put the phone back in its cradle. I liked everything about Cuzco—the architecture, the climate, and the people, who wore traditional dress and were quiet and calm. We had watched the procession at the cathedral before boarding the train, with women carrying silver trays with their baby Jesus figures to be blessed by the priest before being taken home to add to the crèche. A magical morning, and now we were headed to what we imagined would be the highlight of an already amazing trip.

For some reason I've never known, we were given the two front seats in the first car of the train to Machu Picchu. This train is largely devoted to transporting tourists to this most important historical site and thus is designed to maximize the view, and we had the best seats in the house, so our view was unobstructed and expansive.

As the train left the city and traveled through the residential areas surrounding it, our progress was slow. Several times the train stopped for a few minutes, while people or horses or a truck made their way across the tracks. I didn't mind, because that gave me time to observe the homes and small farms alongside the railway.

These homes were small, with dirt yards and ramshackle out-buildings housing tools, animals, and who knows what else. Some of the yards ran right up to the tracks, with no fencing or protective barriers. In most of the yards, I saw people doing chores: men tending horses, women hanging laundry or cooking on outside fires, children carrying firewood or feed. One little girl looked to be about three years old, and she was dressed in a lovely blue dress with ruffles, her hair brushed and beribboned. But she was barefoot and carrying a huge basket filled with vegetables over to where her mother was cooking. A little boy argued with a goat over their destination, and so far the goat was winning.

And I, with my Western postindustrial bias, thought, *Why are these people working? It's Christmas morning.* Well, of course, they were working. The chores of a farm life don't rest on Christmas morning. The animals must be fed and moved; the fire must be stoked; the bread baked; the laundry hung; the fence repaired. The rhythms of life continue day by day. And the work flows through it. I imagine that they attended church that day or gathered with family to celebrate, but I don't know that. I do know they worked, and I do know that I was forced to examine my ideas about the role and place and meaning of work. What a gift that was! My life has been better for it.

Before that Christmas morning, I had never had cause to consider that I held biases about work; they were at least in part determined by my culture and my life experience so far. Work was just work, separate in some way from life in general, and though necessary, valuable, and potentially rewarding, not the heart of things. Work was someplace you went where you did specific tasks for a certain amount of time and then you returned to life, where people loved and argued and played and prayed and where relationships counted. Whatever else work might be for you—drudgery, inspiring, satisfying, discouraging, interesting—it was above all separate from life and therefore from love.

Oh, I knew people who said they loved their work. I was in fact at times one of them. I had in the course of my life before that day done many different jobs. I had been a mortgage banker, a bookstore clerk, a receptionist, an accounting clerk, a maid, a researcher, a teacher, a secretary, and a few other things I can't recall right now. I had asked for and gotten special permission to start work at age fifteen because I wanted to earn my own money and I wanted to be involved in the wider world. In early adulthood, lacking a solid career goal, I had a variety of jobs that I sought based on what I then believed to be the only sensible criteria: hours, salary, advancement potential, stability, and proximity to home. After all, I was also a wife and mother, and work needed to accommodate to those roles.

Most of the jobs I had in those days I thought of as boring. I had learned a good work ethic from my father and from the broader environment I grew up in, so despite being bored, I worked steadily and did as well as I could with any assignment I was given. I thought that the problem was with me since, when I looked around, no one else seemed to be complaining or at least if they were, it was about salary or working conditions or, most often, their unreasonable boss. I really didn't have much of a problem with those things, but I was truly bored. I began to wonder if I might find some career path that would be both challenging and meaningful. I'm not sure how I would have defined those things at that time, but those words were the descriptors that pushed my desire.

And so I went back to school and studied anthropology and philosophy and psychology and found work that I could truly say met the criteria of being both challenging and meaningful. I could begin to say I loved my work. It no longer fit in with my other roles as well, and it wasn't even as financially rewarding as some of my unloved jobs were, but it suited me and gave me rewards that I hadn't known one could get from work.

So when I read then-new ideas in articles and books about finding your passion and following your bliss, I was enthusiastic. I thought this was surely correct and that most people should do that.

Do what you love, and the money will follow. The message traveled far and wide, and I began to hear more and more people expressing it; I felt affirmed in my choices and certain that this was good advice for everyone.

How naïve I was! The fact is that most of the people in this world don't have that choice. Most of the people in my town don't have that choice. They work at the jobs that are available to them given their circumstances. Indeed, many people in the world are unable to find paid work of any kind, and many more people choose for whatever reasons not to go out into the workforce. And yet, when I traveled and when I paid attention at home, I noticed that most of those people seemed content enough, and I came to believe that assuming them unhappy and dissatisfied was the worst sort of presumption on my part.

Yet I knew from my own experience the satisfaction of doing a good job, of taking on a new challenge, of learning and growing in mastery, and of time spent focused on a particular worthwhile goal and the joys of completion and successful goal achievement. So how could it be that people who were denied the opportunities of discovery and choice that I had enjoyed due to geography and other fortunate circumstances were also happy and satisfied in their lives? What did that mean about the role of work in the journey of wholeness?

What I needed was a new definition of work and a grander scheme to place it in. I needed to talk to people and read more books and look more broadly in order to begin to understand. I needed teachers. And gradually over time, I found them and came to see from the stories I was told and witnessed that everything I knew about work was true. I didn't need to discard a theory because it didn't apply to everyone—I needed instead to see the larger themes of meaning and value that work brings to all lives. I needed to see that work can indeed bring purpose and meaning and joy to a life and that all work, from the loftiest to the most menial, adds structure and discipline and testing to shape our characters and forge our self-respect.

We have a human need to contribute. Each of us wants to feel that we matter, that our participation is needed by the whole, whether we are aware of that need or not. Work, whatever form it takes, gives us that opening—the opportunity to do our part. And through it we are made whole and renewed again and again. If in the course of a life, we are given the chance to choose our career and shape our own work life, then we are fortunate indeed. But all of us can choose the way we work. We can choose to see the task before us as an opportunity for self-expression and self-creation, because it always is. The way you do what you do tells the world who you are, and the way you do what you do determines who you will be in the future.

And the answer is always love. Love your work. Love doing the dishes as much as writing a chapter; love cleaning the toilets and walking the dog; love mowing the lawn or flying a jet. Never stop pursuing your dreams, but don't let that become dissatisfaction with now. Now is all we have. This job, this task, this chore, that's all there is. You might as well love them. The fact, the larger truth, the one that isn't told nearly as often as it should be is that you need the work more than it needs you and, at the same time, your contribution is essential to us all.

Do what you love, if you can, but always love what you do. It will show, and it will grow. Love makes more love. Without fail.

I can't end without this little story. I don't know what to make of it, but I'll tell it, and you can decide its meaning. Once, back in the time when I was perpetually dissatisfied with my work, I had a job working as administrative assistant to the president of a national corporation. Our offices were lush and quiet, and the man himself couldn't have been nicer. I earned a good salary. I didn't have much to do each day except be present to answer his calls and keep his calendar and occasionally serve coffee to his visitors. He let me help him plan a major golf tournament for charity. I think he knew I was bored and was being kind.

I complained about this job all the time. All of my friends heard about it, apparently once too often for a dear lady who loved me and wanted me to be happy. Finally, she said, "You should be grateful for that job. And if you don't find a way to be grateful for it, nothing will ever change." I don't know what I said at the time, but I was both offended and intrigued. What if she was right? Of course, she was right on the first count: it was a very good job, and I agreed I should be grateful for it. And what if she was right about my attitude as well? I could see that I was making myself miserable, and I thought I might give it a try, to see if I could find things to be grateful about from that job. So I began to make a list of good things about my job. It was hard at first, but I could do it at work since I didn't have much to do, so I stuck with it, and after a while, the list grew pretty long. And one day I was walking on my lunch hour and realized I was happy and that I loved my job. I actually loved my job. I knew I was really lucky to have it.

Not long after, I got a totally unexpected phone call from someone I had met months before, offering me an interview for a job I had dreamed of and despaired of ever getting. I accepted the interview and then the job. When I gave my two weeks' notice to the nice man at the major corporation, I could say truthfully that I had enjoyed working there and was grateful for the opportunity and all that I learned. I didn't tell him that the main thing I learned was how to love my work.

Work is love made visible. And if you cannot work with love but only with distaste, it is better that you should leave your work and sit at the gate of the temple and take alms of those who work with joy.

—Kahlil Gibran, Lebanese-American artist, poet, and writer

30

SHAKEN ASSUMPTIONS

All the world is my school and all humanity is my teacher.
—George Whitman, American owner, Shakespeare and Company bookshop, Paris

Aside from Paris and the town I live in, India is my favorite place in the world so far. There may be some other place I haven't seen yet, and I'm hopeful that's true. I wouldn't want to think I've already seen the best and everything else will be second-rate in comparison. That will have to wait for now. For now, I have India.

A lot of people are shocked when they hear that I love India, particularly some of those who have been there. It's the kind of place that one loves or hates—there's seldom a lukewarm reaction. Those people who hate it say, "It's dirty, and oh, the poverty, and how about the way they treat women? How can you like it?" And I say, "But, oh, the color, the vitality, the sounds, the smells, the kindness of the people, their dignity, the richness of its history and its art, the way people live their spirituality outdoors and in public all day long. How can you not like it?"

I've come to understand that at least part of what I love is how India forces me to question my assumptions. And I know that to live the way I hope to live, I must never allow my mind to become closed to new ideas or different ones, no matter their age or provenance, and I must always be willing to learn.

India is a fabulous teacher.

Before my first visit, I thought I understood poverty—what it looked like, how it affected people, its causes and effects. My culture has a poverty story, and I accepted it without question. Oh, the tragic poor. They hate the way they live and would give anything to live like the rest of us. They feel bad that they are poor and resent us and feel shame about themselves. Of course the poor commit crimes; they have no hope and no recourse. This is the public version. The silent part of the story, the part that's not spoken but communicated no less effectively, is that it's their fault they are poor—they are shiftless or descended from shiftless people, or they are not as smart or as ambitious or as talented as the rest of us and we'd do well to avoid them. So we don't live near them, we send our children to private schools if we can so they don't come in contact with them, and we try not to make eye contact when we pass them on the street. The theme of this story is shame—theirs for being poor, ours for allowing it and for our unacknowledged pride at not being among their number.

In India, rich people touch poor people, and poor people smile at rich people and even offer to help them if they can. I don't presume to know what people feel or to understand the complexities of their culture, to truly know their poverty story, but I know what I see when I am with them. And what I see is respect that travels from up to down and down to up and across and between people from all walks of life. The toothless, barefoot man who helped me through the throngs at the temple to Shiva's son was sincerely glad to help and smiled with genuine kindness at my well-dressed, educated guide and at me. We all shook hands when we parted. I felt cared for by both of them. Yes, I gave him some money and we bowed *namaste* to each other, but the connection was more than that. We shared for a moment that most precious of all things—respect and compassion. His compassion for me, not mine for him. I was a stranger and confused and a little frightened, and he helped me. That's all, and that's a lot.

In that same temple, a woman offered me milk to share to honor Shiva's sacred bull. The milk was in a brass bowl, from which many others had sipped. I refused, with my Western, probably correct, concerns about sanitation, and I felt guilty for that. I couldn't explain because of the language barrier, and I hated to think I had hurt her feelings. But she absolved me almost before I felt bad. She touched her fingers to my tummy and smiled and bowed and passed the bowl to someone else. I touched her hand in thanksgiving, and she patted my shoulder, and we both passed on in the moving crowd. A moment in time and a universe in empathy, in shared humanity. She knew and I knew, and we understood.

Although India has changed so much since my first visit in 1995—there are no more snake charmers in the streets and New Delhi, although thankfully not Bombay, has even relocated the cows—there are still beggars everywhere, particularly in the big cities and near tourist attractions. One day in Bombay, we were walking along a side street near our hotel, and a girl of about six or seven began to follow us with her hand out. She was dirty and barefoot and beautiful, as only little beggar girls can be. She didn't have any English, and I have no idea what her language was. In India, there are over four hundred nationally recognized languages and over two thousand dialects spoken. We know so little of real diversity here. Anyhow, she and I couldn't talk to each other except with our eyes or in gestures. I shook my head no. Everyone advises not to give money to beggars, advice I rarely follow, but on this morning, I had no coins and no small bills. I sometimes carry hard candies or fruit for this reason, but not this day. We were just out for a morning stroll.

But beggar girls can be persistent, and she followed us still. Our little group—my husband, the child, and me—passed a food stall that sold chips and drinks and sweets, and it occurred to me what I could do. So I approached the vendor and asked the price of orange juice. He answered with a number in rupees that equaled about a quarter US. So I asked for one and handed it to the little girl. Her eyes lit up; she expertly inserted the straw in the box and began to drink. As if from nowhere, about ten little boys and girls materialized around us, all with their hands out. The vendor shook his head, as if to say, "See what you get, dumb American lady," but the little girl and

I smiled, and I handed the vendor the money to pay for everyone's orange juice. Then even the vendor smiled.

The kids stayed with us for a while as we walked. They drank their orange juice and played kick the can and laughed with us—and at me when I took my turn at can-kicking—and finally melted back into the crowd to return to begging, I presume, and to check in with their parents, who are never far away. I admit I don't understand their lives, nor do I know what they suffer in hardship, but I do know that these little people and I connected that morning. We shared a stroll and a smile and a game, and I am grateful for it.

They didn't deserve or want my pity. They wanted money or food and, perhaps even more, to be successful in the job they were assigned. I wanted to participate, to be with them for a moment and to earn the reward of their smiles.

I am sure some would judge my actions and find them problematic. I am fairly positive none of it was politically correct, and perhaps it was not in the ultimate best interests of India or of those children. I don't mind. I am willing to be wrong in the service of love, and I believe that, on that morning for those moments, love was exchanged.

That's why I love India. Love is welcome there. Gifts are given and received across the lines and up and down and all around with joy and respect.

I no longer assume I know anything about the lives of other people who may live differently from me and have different challenges. India taught me that I don't know many of the things I thought I knew. And she also taught me to be on the lookout for opportunities to help, to share, to show respect, and to accept offers of love with joy and simplicity.

I would prefer a thousand mistakes in extravagance of love to any paralysis in wariness of fear.

—Gerald May, American psychiatrist and author

31

HOBBIES

Three grand essentials to happiness in this life are something to do, something to love, and something to hope for.

—Joseph Addison, late seventeenth-century English essayist, politician and poet

Once I met two women in an airport lounge. They were sisters who lived on opposite coasts and were traveling together to attend a convention of couponers. Couponers are people who search out and use manufacturers' and vendors' coupons to save money, often quite a lot of money. But these people, it turns out, don't just look in their local paper or gather discount coupons from mailers. They work hard at searching out coupons from many sources and devise strategies for doubling and tripling and otherwise maximizing each one. It's a skill set and a very time-consuming activity. For devotees, there are local clubs, newsletters, numerous websites, online groups, and regional and national conventions. Most people start out small to save a little money and gradually develop their interest, skill, and involvement until couponing becomes much more than thrift—it becomes a passion. The sisters told me it was their hobby.

Merriam-Webster's Dictionary defines "hobby" as "a pursuit outside one's regular occupation engaged in especially for relaxation." Other definitions include the qualifiers "for fun" or "for pleasure." There is common agreement that the word refers to an activity or interest that is done for pleasure rather than gain, and that hobbies are done in one's "spare" time. There are literally hundreds of activities from which someone might choose a hobby. After meeting the two sisters, I began wondering about hobbies, and not long after, that wonder exploded when I happened to attend, quite by accident, a convention of yo-yoers.

Yo-yoing is a popular pastime of many generations and cultures. I remember yo-yos from childhood, but I had no idea the game was still popular or had any kind of following at all until I happened to stay at a hotel where the World Yo-Yo Convention, sponsored by the International Yo-Yo Federation, was being held. I was in this town for the American Psychological Association's annual meeting. Since I registered late, the convention hotel was full, and I found a room at a different hotel well within walking distance. When I registered, I noticed an unusual number of young males in the lobby, backpacks bulging and jeans sagging. They chatted with each other and sipped from Styrofoam coffee cups or bottles of energy drinks and seemed intent on whatever they were up to. I asked the front desk clerk what was happening at the hotel and who the young men were. She said, "The International Yo-Yo Convention is here, with several hundred attendees. The competitions will be starting tonight. It's free. You should go. These guys are something."

So I did. And they were. I was utterly fascinated at the skill and the devotion of the practitioners, most of whom were male and under thirty, although there were gender and age exceptions. The grand master was a man in his seventies from Japan, and there was a young woman from Oklahoma who destroyed her opponent in the head-to-head match I watched on the third night. Yes, I attended matches every night and even missed a few of my lectures to follow one of my favorites. And the yo-yos were magnificent, beautifully designed and decorated and personalized. I could see why these people were hooked. If I had stayed one more day, I think I might have started yo-yoing myself just to be part of this excellent crowd.

About this same time, I was at a professional football game with some friends, and again I was struck by the passion of the fans. These people really cared about the game and its outcome. Now, not a fan myself, I had been curious about this for years. Why did all these people spend so much time watching football on TV? Why is Super Bowl Sunday practically a national holiday? Who cares? Don't you people have better things to do with your time? I had tried, really tried, to like football—once for a man, once to fit in with a group I liked a lot, and once just because I thought I must be missing something since so many people loved it. It didn't work. No matter how hard I tried, I just couldn't love it. But the people around me on this Sunday afternoon did. Their engagement was no less real because I couldn't feel it.

Having noticed the couponers, the yo-yoers, and now the football fans, I began to pay attention to the whole spectrum of activities that fall under the headings hobby or leisure activity or pastime, curious to understand the what, who, when, why, and how of it all. Why does Janice love football? Why does Candy spend all that time and money showing her pedigreed dogs? Why does Wayne lock himself into his garage for days on end making things from the discards he collects at yard sales and on walks? Why do I have thousands of books in my house, books that have been moved from home to home at least fifteen times, boxes and boxes full that earned complaints even from professional movers. "Lady, why do you keep these books? Have you read them all? Will you ever read them again?" I might or might not, but that has nothing to do with it. I love them.

And, of course, that's the answer. We, all of us, are creative and passionate and full of love. Creativity, passion, and love all need expression. Hobbies are as vital to our health and well-being as a wholesome diet and exercise. I always ask new clients what their hobbies are. The answers tell me more than almost anything about who they are and how they are doing and where our work will be. Sometimes the hobby helps me know the person better right away—sometimes it hides more than it reveals, but still points the way to better understanding. Every once in a while, the answer tells me about loss, about depression, about a life on hold. Always the answer is a guide in the journey to self.

Our hobbies are part of the way we answer life's perennial questions: Who am I? Where do I belong? What matters? They are for many of us the purest form of self-expression. They name our tribe. They highlight our values. How we spend our time and with whom and doing what, when we have clearly and unambiguously chosen our participation, is one of the surest signs of our personhood at its core. I am a person who loves stories, and I read books, watch movies, and go to plays—for relaxation, for pleasure, for entertainment, but even more, to express myself, that is, because doing so is authentic for me. When I am engaged with a story, I am for that moment being precisely me. I'm not doing it for money, for prestige, for honor, or for any of the myriad motivators that drive many of my actions. I'm simply being the person I am, and it fully engages me. I like talking about stories, researching stories, telling stories, and hearing stories. I'm willing to give lots of energy to stories, and it doesn't make me tired.

The coupon sisters told me they looked forward to the annual convention all year long. It was the one time of the year that they could focus their energy on their hobby and share their excitement with others who felt the same. They said they had met the nicest people at these sessions and developed many friendships. And this camaraderie went with them all year, imagining a coupon friend's delight at finding a great value or the tiny frisson of competitive pride when they caught a big one. Their eyes sparkled. One of the sisters said, "I bet you think we're crazy, spending this much time on something like this. In fact, the trips probably cost everything we save, but we get so much pleasure from doing it." I said, "No, I don't think you're crazy at all. In fact, just the opposite, I'm pretty sure it's a sign of mental health."

And I do think that. Hobbies are both a sign of mental wellness and a pathway to it. They are so critical to our well-being, I think we should find a new name, one that elevates them to their appropriate standing. Maybe we should call them expressions or revelations, or use the synonym "avocation," which comes from the Latin and means something close to *call away from*. I like that. Our hobbies call us away from all that is external, from the world out there, and bring us back to ourselves and then out again to express and connect from someplace within.

For the good life, we need something to do, something to love, and something to hope for. Find things to be passionate about and do them. Don't worry if what you like is different from your friends or family, and don't worry if you don't like what they like. This is the place where one must be entirely one's self. That's the purpose; that's the gift. Go all in. Wear the T-shirt; buy the hat. Don't hold back. Who knows? The world needs your enthusiasm as much as you need to have it. If it hadn't been for the coupon sisters and the yo-yo boys, I might have never discovered the freedom to be me—silly, impractical, passionate, buried in books, joyous me.

It is the creative potential itself in human beings that is the image of God.

—Mary Daly, American feminist philosopher and theologian

32

THE RIGHT QUESTION

No one is dumb who is curious. The people who don't ask questions remain clueless throughout their lives.

—Neil deGrasse Tyson, American astrophysicist

We met Norm when we were on a group tour of Southeast Asia visiting Viet Nam, Cambodia, and Thailand. Not exactly a budget tour, it was still a large group that mostly traveled by bus to take in the sights and from city to city. The official group itinerary was twenty-one days, so we were with these people—total strangers one and all—for a long time. It wasn't our first time on a group tour, so we knew what to expect and, for the most part, how to accommodate.

Mark and I love to travel and have taken all types of trips over the years, but we much prefer individual travel. We like to plan our own itinerary and to be able to change it on a whim. The structure of organized travel easily becomes too tight for us, and frankly, I am too much of an introvert to want to spend that much time with people I don't know and will likely never see again. The last time we made such a trip, I told Mark, "Well, okay, I'll go, but *I will not say good morning to those people every day!*"

However, there are times and places when a group is by far the best way to travel, and this was one of those. Language, logistics, and time limits all pointed to the advantages of having someone else coordinate and facilitate our movement. So we booked it and began planning how to balance our preferences with the natural order of things (a little like life, don't you think?).

The trip originated in Bangkok, a favorite city of ours from previous trips. We love the Oriental Hotel on the Chao Phraya River, and the group was staying elsewhere, so one of our adjustments was to arrive early and spend a few days there first. Paradise. Breakfast on the river patio is heaven and, I believe, is the world's best treatment for jet lag. Afterward, we would hop a water taxi and go upriver to the City Palace or to visit the reclining Buddha and come back for Thai massage in the hotel spa, another slice of heaven.

So, jet lag over and thoroughly shifted into life in Asia mode, we met up with our tour group at their hotel and set out to see Thailand. The first morning we all boarded the bus, scrambled around for seats and space for our bags and packages, said hello to each other, and settled back to listen and learn. One of the things I do like about group travel is the stories the tour guides tell. I'm never sure if they are completely factual—indeed, I think they often aren't—but they nevertheless are entirely true in that they convey meaning. They help me understand the culture and the history of the place I've come to and give me ideas and questions to explore further on my own and from other sources.

On this first morning, our guide began talking about the history and culture of Thailand and the city of Bangkok, much of which was familiar to me, but not to most of my fellow travelers. People had questions, and our guide, a Thai gentleman named Krit who would be with us throughout the journey, patiently answered. I noticed that one particular man asked quite a lot of questions. He was most concerned with details of the plans for the day and then for subsequent days. I thought some of his questions might be premature, but they didn't bother me. However, I noticed some signs of impatience from other people—eye rolls, twitches, and mumbles.

Over the course of that first day and during dinner that night—the first and only dinner we ate with the group; one of our accommodations is to skip group meals whenever possible—we met many of the people in our group. They were mostly over-fifty couples, but there were a few singles and a few younger people, even one pair of honeymooners in their twenties. Most were from the United States, but there were also four Brits, four Chilean women, and the honeymooners were from Tasmania. They were all nice people and fine to share a meal with in Bangkok. The man with all the questions was named Norm, and he was from California, traveling alone, something he said he did at least once a year to different parts of the world.

Group tour days follow a definite rhythm, particularly on days when the group travels from hotel to hotel, city to city. There's a time for bags to be outside your room so they can be collected and a time to meet in the lobby to board the bus. In between, you are supposed to tend to your personal needs and consume any sustenance you think you will need to meet the day (for me, the pressure is to drink enough coffee to get me going in a time frame when I would normally drink one—I'm a sipper). Oddly, most people manage to get these things done on time, and the process moves along smoothly enough. On this trip, the honeymooners were occasionally late, but we all politely ignored that, and it was fine.

As the days passed, Norm continued to ask more questions than anyone else—lots more questions than anyone else. By about day five, his questions had begun to elicit a major response from the group. I don't know if he noticed, but many of our companions would share looks and comments with each other, the eyes would roll, the papers would rattle, and the tension built. I became unsettled, fearful of a confrontation, embarrassed for Norm, and yet, as impatient with him as everyone else.

And then my husband, dear Mark, spoke up and said in a clear, calm, and curious voice, "Norm, why do you ask so many questions?"

And Norm replied, "Because I want to know what's going to happen next."

And Mark said, "That makes sense."

And that was that. No more tension, no more impatience, no more negativity. We traveled together for sixteen more days, Norm asked his questions, we all reaped the benefits of the answers, and we said goodbye at the end. I didn't learn to love group travel—the structure is still a little tight for me and being with so many people tiring—but I did learn a lot about honesty and respect and how the right question at the right time is what love sometimes looks like. Of course, it's only ever the right question if it's posed with genuine interest and respect and without agenda. That's Mark. He just naturally knows some things about life that I've been working hard to learn. I sure am grateful I get to travel with him.

My religion is very simple. My religion is kindness.

—Dalai Lama XIV, Tibetan Buddhist spiritual leader

33

THE POWER OF POSSIBILITY

Live out of your imagination, not your history.

—Stephen Covey, American educator, author, and businessman

Without imagination, nothing new can happen. We remain stuck in whatever patterns or loops we have inhabited up to now. To move forward, to grow, to change and evolve, we must first imagine a different course or at least imagine that one exists whether we can see it yet or not.

Years ago, my husband and I were looking for a new house to buy. We had moved from a rental in the city to home ownership in the suburbs for good, practical reasons—we could get more house for the money (true); less crime (not really); quieter (true, but we forgot that we like the energy of the city even if it is a little noisier); and the commute wouldn't be awful (it was awful). We realized quickly that we had made a mistake and began the process of house-hunting all over again.

The city neighborhoods that we liked were known to be pricey. Per square foot prices were at least twenty-five percent more than in the suburbs and could go as high as fifty percent higher. So we began our search with the attitude that we would adjust downward. We would give a little on neighborhood and go to our second or third choice, and we would accept a smaller house with fewer amenities to try to get a home we could afford in the location we wanted.

Both of us enjoy looking at houses and driving around our favorite neighborhoods, so the idea of the home search didn't fill us with dread, and we had already made our attitude adjustment, so we began in good spirits. Five weeks and about fifty houses later, our attitudes, along with our physical endurance, were flagging. Still, we left on a Saturday morning with no appointments set and no houses identified to see. We thought we would just drive around and see if we could find any for-sale-by-owners or open houses that we had missed. I might note here that this was before the Internet, so house-hunting was a much more hands-on activity. You actually met realtors in their offices and looked through listing books or drove around and tried to spot "For Sale" signs in people's yards.

Our favorite neighborhood was one with homes mostly built between 1890 and 1920, Victorian or Craftsman in style, on gorgeous heavily wooded lots, right in the very heart of the city and surrounding the city's largest park. Like many in-town areas, this neighborhood was dotted with multifamily properties, a few small apartment complexes, and the occasional fixer-upper or newer construction with little charm. We thought we might settle for one of the newer, smaller homes just to live where we wanted to live, so we began the grid search of the neighborhood, driving street by street, looking for signs. When we saw one, we would jot down the phone number of the owner or the listing agent so we could call and ask the price. Usually one of us would say, "That one's nice, but we can't afford it." We had drawn the same conclusion about every house we'd seen and liked throughout our search.

We pulled up in front of a house that was simply gorgeous, a two-story Craftsman on one of the best streets, with a small, manicured front lawn, a gracious front porch, and two giant old oak trees standing guard on either side. The sign in front said, "Open House, Come on in!" My husband said, "Well, I know we can't afford this, but let's go take a look anyway. It's a beautiful house." It *was* a beautiful house, with high ceilings, original fireplaces, and wide, natural wood moldings. Each room was spacious and interesting in its own way. I was entranced and walked through thinking something like, *Oh, I wish I could afford this.*

We found the fact sheet the realtor had left in the home, which included the price, and I was right—the asking price was well outside our maximum. Neither of us was surprised, so then, not disappointed, but I think we both felt a little regret that we would not be able to make this house our home.

Back in the car, I decided to take another look at the flyer we'd found in the house, and I noticed for the first time that it mentioned a carriage house in back that was currently rented, with income in a certain amount. I didn't say a word to Mark, but pulled out my calculator, which went with us everywhere at that time, and I began to run the numbers. I ran them a few times, not daring to believe what I was seeing.

I suggested we stop for coffee and talk about what we'd seen. Mark agreed, and we drove to our favorite coffee shop and found a table outside. I said, "I may be wrong and I want you to check me, but I think we can afford that house we just saw." He looked doubtful, but I gave him the numbers, and he did his own calculations. I saw his face change, and he looked at me and said, "I think you're right. The rental unit out back makes it completely affordable. We can do it."

We did.

We were so happy in that house. And it only happened because somehow I got a glimpse that what was impossible might be possible. It would have been so easy to stay in the "we can't afford it" rut we were in and drive away, not looking back. Neither of us had ever owned rental property or even considered it before that day. Nor were we very sophisticated about real estate investment or money management for that matter. I can't say today why I was able to spot that moment of possibility, but I can say with certainty that seeing the possibility changed everything.

I love remembering that. I loved that moment, and I loved the gifts that moment brought me. One of those gifts was the awareness that imagination is the agent of change. That's no less true in my quest for wholeness than it was in the house search. If I can't imagine a better life for myself, I won't get one. If I can't imagine myself a more moral or loving person, I won't be one.

Likewise, often my principal function as a therapist or as a friend is to see and hold the power of possibility when the other person can't. A person who is suffering from any cause or for any reason can only see a portion of what is and little of what might be. There is something in the pain that blocks the view. I know that, and still, when I encounter loss or injury, I too for that time can only see dimly those bits of reality outside the perimeter of my pain. In those times, I need a helper, an ally, someone who can hold onto possibility when I can't.

It is never my job to define or even describe the possibilities, because that too easily becomes advice at best or condescension at worst, and also, I would be wrong. I do not know what is possible for someone else. I do know that possibility exists and that even the tiniest welcome can be enough to fire the imagination and open the door to the power of possibility.

Imagination is everything. It is the preview of life's coming attractions.

—Albert Einstein, German-born theoretical physicist

PART IV

February
A month in St. Simons

"The ocean is the place where I re-balance my life and remember what's important."

FAITH

GRACE

Grace: unmerited divine assistance given humans
for their regeneration or sanctification; approval, favor;
a charming or attractive trait; sense of propriety or right.

—*Merriam-Webster Dictionary*

Some people say that happiness is an inside job, that it's up to each person to create his or her own happiness. Some even seem to infer that it's simply a decision we can make. Abraham Lincoln famously said that we are all as happy as we make up our minds to be. There's truth in that of course, but like so many statements, only a partial truth or a truth that points the way but barely touches on the reality. Yes, we are responsible for our own happiness as well as our own healing and growth, and it is necessary to make that decision—to decide to take responsibility for our lives—but beyond that, we must then do all the hard work that implementing that decision requires.

It begins with knowing and accepting ourselves, digging down beneath the layers of denial, distortion, and rejection to the essential truths of our being, and then finding a place in the real world for that knowledge. We must discover who we are, become who we are, and fall in love with that person. We must create a life within which that person can thrive, and to do so, much will need redemption. We will have to find ways to forgive ourselves and forgive others, and we will need to revisit old wounds until we can find a healing for them.

To do that, we will need to be powered by love. Only love can bring forth the energy and resolve that is required to stay the course and do the work of forgiveness and acceptance. We have to find a way to love ourselves and to express love in the world, no matter how frightening that may at first appear. Love heals. It's as simple as that and as complicated. Love heals, but making ourselves available for love can be another matter entirely. Sometimes we hide or run or give up and become bitter. It can indeed seem entirely too difficult, this pressure to take full responsibility for our own path.

On my path of wholeness, I have done all of those things: I've run, hidden, and almost given up from the sheer magnitude of the task of becoming. Each time that I went for therapy, even the last, when much had been healed already, it was because the job was too big for me. I needed help, and I knew that. Asking for help was never easy for me; I had extracted from the environment of my early years a belief that it was all up to me, that asking for help was both un- acceptable and pointless. I was reared in an atmosphere that valued independence and distrusted others, and I not only accepted that, I couldn't imagine an alternative universe. So far as I could tell, it was the truth of the world. So when life was too much for me, I sol- diered on and usually made things worse, and only in desperation sought help and then only from professionals. I created a hard path for myself.

If only I had known then about grace, how much softer my life would have been!

Grace is the movement of goodness in the universe. I have ideas about where it comes from, and I know that other people have their own ideas and some even a sense of certainty. I am only certain of the reality of grace and that it flows with or without my belief or recog- nition. My job is simply to pay attention, to stand still, hold out my hands, and accept it when it comes. My work is to stay open and be attentive and perhaps to say a prayer of gratitude.

Grace, like love, can't be willed, and it can't be earned. The very definition of the word includes the phrase "free and unmerited favor," and while often used in association with a specific reference to "God," grace also means favor, privilege, clemency, charm, a pleasing appearance or quality of movement. It can be a prayer, a sense of propriety, or a quality of consideration, thoughtfulness. The term "grace notes" refers to notes that are added to a musical piece that, while not essential to its integrity, give it color or added meaning.

My life has been filled with grace notes. As it turns out, it was never all up to me, and I was never in it alone. Grace flowed even when I couldn't recognize it. How much nicer when I can! Sometimes grace looks like kindness or attention or an unexpected boon. Sometimes it's in the way the wind blows or the sea shades into the sky or the bluebird sings outside the window. Sometimes it's in shared laughter or the smile of a stranger. Other times it's the insight that comes from nowhere and changes not just my thinking, but even the way I live in the world. Grace can be in the grandest of things and the infinitesimal. In whatever form, it always flows. I can choose to move in that flow and be grateful for it. So I guess Abraham Lincoln was right after all—I am just about as happy as I make up my mind to be. I just need to do the work and open myself to grace.

If we turn our mind toward the good, it is impossible that little by little the whole soul will not be attracted thereto in spite of itself.

—Simone Weil, French philosopher and author

34

PSYCHOTHERAPY 5
THE WISE WOMAN

I trust the tempo of my unfolding.

—Julia Cameron, American author and artist

Years after my therapy with Harold, though it's surprising how few those years were considering how much had changed, I had been reborn. I had a new, beloved husband—one who knew how to love and who loved me, me in the particular, the actual person that I am. And whom I loved in the same way. My daughters were launched and traveling their own paths. I had a new career that enriched me and challenged me and made me be better than I am all the time. I had learned when to let go and when to hold on and how to do both. I had forgiven myself for most of it and also forgiven most of them, the ones who had hurt me and frightened me and left me. I had been given a new relationship to mystery and to the real world that worked pretty well much of the time.

But I knew I had a lot left to learn. And it occurred to me that, in order to do that, I needed a crone. In the ancient stories, the tales that have endured and held their shape because of intrinsic human value, the crone is the image of the wise woman, the one who, by virtue of her travels on the journey of life and her attention along the way, has acquired a deep and fervent wisdom. It is to the crone that one goes to be introduced to the mysteries.

But on a more mundane level, I also knew that my pride might stand in the way of the needed lessons with a person my age or younger. It's important in this life to know what your limits are.

So I went looking. I looked first among my acquaintances and friends, and though I found some candidates there, there were reasons why they could not or would not be my teachers. One day I was in Harold's office for one of our now occasional appointments, and I told him what I thought I needed.

He said, "Oh, yes, you should call Paula."

Paula, it turns out, was a Jungian therapist a few years older than me and many years wiser. Our first conversation was by phone, when she explained to me how her practice worked. She said that she was able to offer every-other-week appointments at an agreed-upon, regular time and that if an appointment were missed, it usually could not be rescheduled. However, she said, she had a waiting list that she expected would take about nine months to mature, and she wondered if I felt I could wait that long, assuming I agreed to the terms of her practice. I said, "Yes, I'll wait, and yes, I agree."

I could wait. I had already had my first crone lesson. Crones are not, as I still was, so constantly eager to please. They have limits and rules and preferences, and they communicate them clearly and without apology. *Wow*, I thought, *maybe I can do that, too. What would that even feel like?* I wanted to know.

Several months did pass, and then she called and said she had an opening for a specific time—3:10 p.m. on alternate Thursdays. *Isn't that wonderful?* I thought that then, and I still do. Her clarity and her self-care made me feel safe. Here was a woman I didn't have to take care of, a rarity in my experience, and one who could be trusted to keep her promises.

The day arrived for our first appointment. I arrived at 3:00 p.m.—could she really have meant 3:10 p.m.? She did. I didn't know what to expect. This was before the Internet, so I didn't have any way of seeing an image of her before our meeting. Her waiting room was typical of most doctors' offices—neat but bland, a little on the masculine side, I thought, and it didn't provide many clues to the mystery within. And as I sat, I began to think of the image of the crone as it's often portrayed in myths and fairy tales: the ancient stooped figure dressed in black with a walking stick and a hooked nose. Would my crone look like this? What would the modern version be?

When the door opened and a voice called my name, I looked up to see a lovely, elegant lady dressed in soft colors, with neatly styled long brown hair and clear skin. I saw her as tall, but she wasn't. There was something in her bearing that elevated her. I've called her a "lady," knowing she and others might prefer me to use "woman," but there was and is something profoundly ladylike about her. You just look at her and see good manners and kindliness. She couldn't hide them if she tried.

Of course, she doesn't try, because crone that she is, she's comfortable being exactly who she is. Even in a professional subculture that values equality and creative self-expression and pushes against the old forms that reflect patriarchal hegemony, where calling yourself "woman," not "lady," is worn like tribal markings, Paula continues to look like a lady.

My second crone lesson was complete. A crone doesn't look like you expect her to; she looks like herself. Oh, she was also a woman, strong and powerful and self-defining, but unfazed by fashion and trend, courageous enough to embody the better qualities of womanhood like kindness and good manners that others were willing to leave behind in their quest for empowerment.

She was also wise and smart, which are not the same. She was wise enough to hold still and wait and smart enough to stay two or three or ten steps ahead of my often convoluted thinking. She never judged or condemned or approved either, but instead tilted the mirror slightly so I got a different view or added the missing color to my rainbow. I came to know that I could take a thing to her, some concern or heartache or dream, and she would find a way to surprise me. Just when I thought I had looked at something from every possible angle, she would say something, some odd thing, and I would see it brand-new. Paula understood that mythos healed in a way that Logos never could. She helped me connect my stories to the mythic story from whence they came and from whence their meaning shone.

That was many years ago now. With Paula, I have grown a spine and a heart, and I have learned to be taught by the symbols. We are both older now, and she still has much to teach me and I have much more to learn. I am delighted about that because one of the things that I've learned from her is that the journey is the point of the whole thing. There is no destination; there is only the travel. It's how we do that that matters, and it's there we find our treasure and create our joy. We go in mystery, and mystery enfolds us. Answers give birth to questions, and finding inspires seeking. That's the sum and the secret. Journey on.

The value of myth is that it takes all the things you know and restores to them the rich significance which has been hidden by the veil of familiarity.

—C. S. Lewis, English author, academic, and Christian philosopher

35

IMAGINATION

Logic will get you from A to Z; imagination will get you everywhere.
—Albert Einstein, German-born theoretical physicist

Not too long ago, I had a conversation with an acquaintance about, in a general way, our plans for the future. He talked about the promotion he was in line for and the money he needed to save for his children's education. He said he hoped to travel more someday and have more time for reading and sports. I told him that I planned to keep writing and seeing clients and living as gracious and generous a life as I could manage. I think we both told the truth, but as I drove home, I wondered what each of us had not said. What were his secret dreams, and for that matter, what were mine?

Our biggest secrets are not, as one might think, our deepest shames, but our most precious dreams. We hold them tight, guarding them from the carelessness of others and from our own fears and self-denial. We know with our inner wisdom that dreams must be treated with the tenderest care so as not to be tarnished or diminished until we are ready for their emergence.

And yet, all change begins in the imagination. If we can't envision a different life, a better future, we are not likely to find one. As a therapist, one of my most critical functions is to offer glimpses of possible worlds my clients might inhabit one day. It is never my job to describe those worlds in detail. That is the job of fiction writers and moviemakers and other kinds of dreamers, without whom we would all live smaller lives.

No, my job is to listen carefully for the hidden dreams and then illuminate just a tiny moment from them so that the client can see what's been curtained before and make use of it to create the best next thing for themselves. They didn't teach this in any class or lecture I attended, nor did I read it in a textbook or scholarly tome. I learned this from the teachers and healers who have done that for me.

I became a therapist because one of those healers, a kind and wise man who knew me well and listened carefully, said five words to me when I was struggling after I gave up hope of being a professional anthropologist. He said, "You could be a therapist." I said, "No, it would require too much education, too much time, too much inner work, too much money, too much effort, and I am discouraged, disappointed, and exhausted." He said he knew that and left it at that.

I didn't feel any different when I left him that day. I didn't have more energy or more hope. I felt no less discouraged than when I arrived. But a funny thing happened. Over the days and weeks that followed, I found myself imagining a future for myself. I remembered that once upon a time, I had dreamed of being a psychiatrist. I began to see in my mind's eye the office I would have. I could see the curtains gently blowing from the breeze through the open window. I saw chairs and bookcases and people talking, and I felt some speck of how it might feel to connect with someone in that unique way.

I know this because I kept a journal during that time and I wrote it all down. I also wrote all the reasons I couldn't do it and wrote as well about what I would do instead. Out in the world, I continued to do what I had been doing—going to work, loving my children, taking care of home and health, and exploring my options. One day that exploration took me to a conference being held at a local hotel, mainly to meet a friend from out of town who was attending. There I met a man who was opening a new psychiatric facility in town. We talked about his new venture, and I mentioned I might like to work in that field. I met my friend and enjoyed the visit and didn't think anything more about it.

A few months later, the man called me and offered me a job as his assistant. He wanted me to help him write policies and procedures and set up his databases, all tasks a good, well-trained anthropological researcher could do. I accepted. So there I was—going to work every day with mental health professionals of all types, watching what they did and listening to them talk, and also meeting the patients, hearing their stories and seeing them change.

The rest, as they say, is history. What seemed impossible became, in imperceptible increments, possible, then likely, then done. It was everything I thought it would be—expensive, time-consuming, and hard (very, very hard) physically, mentally, and emotionally . . . and worth every bit of it. It didn't happen smoothly or in a straight line, but it happened. First the quest for credentials to work at the counselor level, then more education, then work at a higher level, then the PhD with all that that requires, internship, postdoc, research, theses. By this time, though, it no longer seemed like work at all. I was in love, and love carried me through.

Well, love, yes, but it started with imagination and would have been impossible without a constant stream of grace, beginning with the gift of the moment when those five words spoken by my thoughtful counselor seeded my imagination. Imagination initiates change and also ignites the fire that powers the movement forward. Einstein said, "Imagination will get you everywhere." I think that might be true. I know for sure that it's where it begins and that nothing much happens without it. It's the spark, and it's the fire. We still have to do the work, but with love and grace, imagination guides us to what's good and right and true.

I am certain of nothing but of the holiness of the Heart's affections and the truth of Imagination.

—John Keats, English Romantic poet

36

HUMOR

A person without a sense of humor is like a wagon
without springs. It's jolted by every pebble on the road.

—Henry Ward Beecher, American clergyman and abolitionist

Humor is good medicine: it adds joy and zest to life, enhances creativity, reduces stress, and improves mood. When we laugh with someone, the bond with that person grows stronger, and we tend to associate more fond memories with him or her. Good research shows that the ability to laugh at the ups and downs of life, to take things in stride, and to laugh at ourselves promotes health and well-being in all its forms.

Why then do we take ourselves so seriously?

I find that my own personal mental health at any given moment precisely correlates with my ability to laugh at myself. If I can see my mistake or my vulnerability as amusing, I am not so devastated by it, and I can move on with something like ease and grace. If for whatever reason, I imbue this moment or this action with somber significance, I am sloping toward melancholy. My momentary failure becomes my identity and my fate, and my mood hurries to meet that assessment.

One time I was invited to speak at a gathering of about fifty or sixty people on a topic dear to my heart and with the assurance that my audience was in tune with my ideas. Pretty nonthreatening scenario, it would seem. However, at that time in my life, I was taking myself pretty seriously, and I was terrified of public speaking. Before the lecture was to begin, I was waiting with my dear friend Evelyn, who had come along to support me, and I was regaling her with my fears. I fortunately don't recall exactly what I said—I'm sure it would be embarrassing to remember—but I do remember what she said after enduring my complaints for a long time. She said, "Oh, dear God, you are not that important." And I laughed.

I was still scared when I walked up to the podium, but not as scared, and I got through the talk just fine. I did notice that most of the people weren't paying that much attention and that the ones who were, were mostly smiling their encouragement.

I've never forgotten that day. I have had many opportunities to speak in public since then, and I've learned a lot about the fear of public speaking, including the fact that it's the number one most common fear. I've learned a lot about effective public speaking, including the principle that when you can focus on the audience rather than yourself, not only do you give a better talk, but your fear is less crippling. Still, by far the most important lesson I've ever gotten, I got that day when my friend helped me laugh at myself.

I know now that my seriousness about myself was related to my lack of self-acceptance. I had not yet decided to choose me. I still hoped that other people could assure me of my worth and my value and that, if I could only earn their approval, I would then be okay. Which also meant that if they didn't approve, I was not okay. That's pretty high stakes when your self-acceptance is dependent upon the acceptance of a room full of people you don't know. No wonder I was scared.

Somewhere along the way, with lots of effort and lots of help, I began to know that my self-acceptance couldn't be contingent and that I would need to learn to be my own friend even when I failed and when no one else was standing with me. I would have to be willing to love and care for myself no matter what. Even if I gave a really bad talk and nobody liked it.

And then, of course, that happened. I let myself get talked into giving a talk at a national conference on a topic that I was fairly well informed about, but that I didn't have a lot of enthusiasm for. I didn't love it. While I could recognize in the abstract its importance, it didn't have personal force for me. But my boss wanted me to do the talk, and I agreed. My preparation was thorough and the content worthwhile. The day came. My session was scheduled by the organizers of the meeting for the last hour of the last day of a three-day conference. So, of course, I was doomed from the beginning. About forty people showed up, and I made my way to the podium and began. We were all bored. I lost my train of thought a few times and referred to my notes more than I usually do. My voice shook and my knees trembled. I knew it was bad, and I knew the best I could hope for was to get it over with without passing out. I finished; they applauded listlessly and hurried out to make their way home.

It was awful. I felt terrible and began rehearsing my failure and pestering myself with doubts and worries. Would I get fired? Could I ever speak again? What were they saying about me? Now this conference took place in a Western state three thousand miles from home, and the plans were for me to continue on to visit a referring psychiatric facility in another Western state with our marketing manager, who had attended my talk. She was witness to my failure, and she didn't like me much to begin with.

So here I am, three thousand miles from home traveling with someone who doesn't like me and who has been present for my big flop, and I need to go and be professional and positive with a group of people I don't know, from whom my employers hope to get continued business. Since we are on the move and cell phones haven't been invented yet, I can't even call my support people. I am completely alone.

And I made the revolutionary decision to be nice to myself. I just did. I was sitting on the plane next to the marketing manager, imagining her disdain for me (I don't think it was completely imaginary), and I thought, *Oh, well, can't be helped. I'll just treat myself like I matter. And*, I thought, *I'm not that important, and neither is this failure of mine. No matter what happens next, I choose me.*

We got through the marketing call okay. I genuinely liked some of the people I met and felt we had common missions for helping clients. I was curious about their work and enthralled with their desert locale. I learned some things and ate a few good meals at their expense. And at some point, I spoke with my people—the ones who do love me no matter what and who tried to assure me it hadn't gone as badly as I thought. Even though they were wrong about that, it felt good to hear, and I felt good to know I was loved. My boss never said anything about my failed performance, so I can't say what she heard or didn't hear. I just told her it fell sort of flat and I wished I had done better, both true.

I'd be less than honest if I said that experience wasn't painful. It was. It took all of my courage to face the next thing and take the next step and not undermine myself by making excuses or seeking affirmation. I just walked on in the pain, paid careful attention to my needs for food and rest and kindness, and sought engagement with the holy present.

I can laugh about it now. It is pretty funny how big a deal I made of a thing that was of so little actual importance. The boss sold the business and went on to other things, but not before I had left to begin my private practice. I don't know what happened to the marketing manager. I never attended that particular conference again, but I'll bet they've had other bad talks if they even continued. What is a big deal, though, for me is what I learned—that I could stand for myself even when I fail, and that failure is sometimes inevitable if you try.

Life is so much easier when we can learn to take ourselves less seriously. I try really hard at most of what I do, but I often fail and make mistakes. It's my magical magnifying mind that makes those mistakes into disasters or symptoms of my overall worthlessness. They are in fact just mistakes, a dime a dozen, and not exclusive to me. Everyone who tries makes them. And as Evelyn told me all those years ago, I'm just not that important. Most people won't even notice, and the few who do will probably forgive me—and if they don't, so what? This great big wonderful world can tolerate my stumbles, and so can I. Humor helps me do that.

At the height of laughter, the universe is flung into a kaleidoscope of new possibilities.

—Jean Houston, American scholar, philosopher, and author

37

LAUGHTER

Laughter is the sun that drives winter from the human face.

—Victor Hugo, French poet and novelist

Once, Mark and I were staying at the Taj Mahal Palace hotel in Bombay (officially Mumbai, but absolutely no one in the city calls it anything but Bombay) at the beginning of a trip to India, our third time in that endlessly fascinating country. This legendary hotel is located on Apollo Bunder right across from the Gateway of India and the harbor. It's a glorious hotel, one of our favorites in the world, not least because of its place in the life of the city. This area of Bombay is abuzz with activity all day and well into the night, but the life within this hotel is nothing like the life on the streets outside. Inside, it's a dignified vitality spiced with the quiet hum of business being done, deals being forged, and occasions celebrated. This is the place where Mumbai's businesspeople hold important meetings, its elite come for high tea in the Sea Lounge, and also where they host their weddings, which the hotel handles with "flawless aplomb," according to their advertising as well as the comments I heard from guests in the hallways and elevators.

Our visit coincided with wedding season in this region of India, so there were weddings at the hotel daily. Now, in India, weddings are major events in the life of a family. A typical wedding consists of several major events over a period of days, ending with the marriage ceremony itself. They are often lavish affairs, which for less affluent families can consume much of the family's wealth. People go all out. And that includes the guests. While some dress in Western clothing, this is the time for women to wear their most beautiful saris, often their own wedding sari, and men to don traditional attire. The overall effect is stunning.

So here we are at the hotel in our comfortable and useful travel clothes, with all these gorgeously dressed people moving along the hallways and lounging in the lobbies. The wedding venues themselves are on two or three mezzanine floors between the lobby and public areas and the guest room floors of the historic wing of the hotel, where our room was located. After dinner, we ambled along the shopping gallery inside the hotel, as much to enjoy being with the people as to window-shop the exquisite and exquisitely expensive treasures displayed. Finally it was time to head up to our room, and we boarded the elevator. My husband said to me, "Did you see all those drunk Indian women?" Well, I was mortified. Had he not noticed that on the elevator with us were two well-dressed Indian men, perhaps hotel guests, but equally likely there for one of the weddings on the next floor? I was so afraid my husband had inadvertently insulted one of the men. India is in most ways a very traditional country, and the standards for women's behavior are very high or very restrictive, depending on your point of view.

One of the Indian men looked my husband in the eye and said, in flawless English, "If you'd like to see some more, come with me! There are lots of them at my wedding." And he laughed. He smiled and waved as he left us on the elevator. We didn't accept his invitation, but I think now we should have.

What could have been a tense moment and might have been with another man or in another place became a joy and treasure to bring home with me and recall with fondness. I smile now as I write this, and think, what a nice man!

Laughter brings us together. It helps us heal, and it helps us relax. There is no better cure for tension or for conflict. It is also a symptom of mental health and a reflection of love. One of the surest ways to know if love is present is to notice if there is laughter.

Not too long ago, one of my clients, Alana, came in and announced that she had just recently fallen in love with her husband of thirty years. For months before that, she had been struggling to unlearn some patterns of behavior set in motion in childhood and carried forward throughout her adulthood that caused her to deny her own needs in favor of those around her. As this realization dawned, her first response was to begin to notice all the people in her life who had gladly accepted her attention to their needs at the expense of her own. One of those people was her husband, and her initial reaction was fury. How could he have ignored her unmet needs all these years when he said he loved her? Didn't he know how much she suffered? How could he be so selfish?

She fumed about this over several sessions, and we returned again and again to an examination of the pattern within her and all the ways it had manifested in her life, including in her relationship with her husband. She made progress in discovering her needs and desires and in learning ways to meet them appropriately day by day. At some point, she came to understand that the needs were hers, and it would be her job to see that they were met, that it probably wouldn't help much to go on blaming others for their failure to do so. After all, she had pretty much kept them secret from everyone, including herself.

As she accepted her responsibility and found ways to be kinder to herself, her anger toward her husband softened, and she began to look at him with what she called "new eyes." These eyes saw a man who had needs of his own and, some of the time, an inability to meet them for himself. Her "old eyes" only looked for ways to make herself valuable to others and, in reality, cared little for the pains and concerns of the other person, despite her constant attempts to please them. So, one day, she said, she asked him a question about himself because she really wanted to understand him better, not in order to please him, but in order to know him.

That question led to several conversations over the course of days and weeks and to a new level of intimacy for them together. She told me that she learned more about him as a person in those few weeks than she had in all their years together. It seems that he was more than willing to open up and talk about his life, with its sorrows and joys, and that he understood that it was not her job to fix it or to make up for it. He was willing to accept that maybe in their time together, he had taken advantage a bit of her willingness to please, and he said he hoped she would give him another chance.

And then he told her a joke, and they laughed out loud, and that's when she fell in love with him. She said that they had always laughed together and that he had charmed her from the first with his good-natured humor. But this new thing, this falling in love, was made possible because now she was laughing with a man she was beginning to know as a separate human being, with needs and failings and gifts and talents of his own, who didn't need her to make him whole and whom she didn't need to make herself whole.

But the icing on the wedding cake was the laughter. This new marriage, the one sanctified by their laughter, would be a marriage based on love and mutual regard. Alana said she had always known that she had chosen the right man for her and that she had never questioned their love for each other, but she had not known that this other love, this new love, would be possible. She had to grow herself into someone who could see with new eyes and who could receive as well as give. She and I both knew that laughter was the grace that carried them through to make time for the growing.

In the sweetness of friendship let there be laughter, and sharing of pleasures. For in the dew of little things the heart finds its morning and is refreshed.

—Kahlil Gibran, Lebanese-American artist, poet, and writer

38

MYSTERY

We have to stop and be humble enough to understand
that there is something called mystery.

—Paulo Coelho, Brazilian lyricist and novelist

A t the end of the day, there are just so many things we can't know. The answer to almost every question that begins with the word "Why?" for example. Why does the sun shine? Or the moon glow? Science, that most fashionable god, offers explanations, but of course, all of science is based on hypothesis testing, and who can say when the hypothesis has been sufficiently tested? Newton was right until he was wrong. So the best we can say with science as our guide is that the current hypothesis tends to suggest that the sun shines because it is actually a ball of fire. Of course, that begs the question of why. Why does a ball of fire shine? And why is the sun a ball of fire? And so on.

Religious people might see the sun as a gift from God or as a god itself. And God divided the heavens and said, "Let there be light," and there was light and it was good. The Brahmans go down to the Ganges and thank the river at sunrise and sunset because they believe that the holy river brings the sun again and again to grow their crops and warm their homes. The Aztecs' primary god was the sun, bringer of life and bounty, to whom they sacrificed virgins to assure his continued blessing.

The rightness or wrongness of a belief and the behaviors it produces bear almost no relation to the strength of its hold on a people or a person. Some beliefs seem foolish, if harmless, and others are downright evil or at least lead to evil acts by their adherents. But no matter how harmful or foolish, beliefs have power precisely because there is so very much we can't know and because we want so badly an explanation for the unknowable. We want to be sure of things.

We want to know what's coming around the bend in the path, what the next day or the next life will hold. We want to know with certainty how we should behave, how we should live our lives. And why wouldn't we? It seems a small enough thing, to want to understand how things work.

And yet, so much remains a mystery. I don't understand the workings of most of the universe, although I think some really dedicated smart people understand a great deal more, and that's good. But I also don't understand, really, why I chose the outfit I'm wearing today or why I live in this town I live in when the world is so huge and interesting or why I love this person and can't tolerate the other person or why I cry when I see an act of great bravery or kindness or when I hear certain songs. Like the scientists, I can make hypotheses about it all and test them out if I want, and I still won't really know. How can there be a cardinal or a baby or a live oak tree or a jellyfish or the northern lights or a llama or Mother Teresa? How can those things happen? Whatever your personal hypothesis, no matter how strongly it may be held, something about that is still a mystery.

So, like it or not, most of it, of this life, is a mystery. And our journey through will be in part characterized by the quality of our relationship to mystery. Whether we struggle or ignore or deny or embrace it. How we understand its operation and its source. And in this, as in so many other things, there are many answers, and my answer will not be yours. You and I may share many beliefs or attitudes, but we won't share all. We may share none, and yet each of us is on exactly the same journey in that we are each trying to work out our understanding based on the lives we've lived so far and the information gathered and perhaps on some inner aspect that is itself a mystery.

Frankly, that delights me. Oh, I used to want all the answers, and I've searched far and wide for convincing formulas and found some that served for a time and then didn't and some that have endured. But finally I got it. I don't want to live in a world that is small enough for me to understand. I want a grander, holier world than any I could possibly describe. And that world must inherently be mostly incomprehensible to me. Thankfully.

What does matter and what I can do something about is the way I encounter mystery when it comes my way. I can choose to meet it with wonder, with awe, with curiosity, even with doubt or skepticism, but always with reverence and the willingness to be present. I can choose to make room for possibility and for hope. I can allow it to enlarge me, to inspire me, and to carry me forward.

My client Sandi told me a story about what happened one day after she left my office when we had been talking about her sadness and pain following the breakup of an important relationship. Sandi is an aerospace engineer and does things with technology that are completely incomprehensible to me, but that she is quite at home with. She isn't affiliated with any organized religion and indeed calls herself agnostic when it comes to faith or a belief in God. She has spent her life working to solve complex problems involving moving machines safely and efficiently through time and space. She likes facts and evidence and doesn't have the luxury of mistakes in her work. So she's inclined toward certainties.

She recalled that the last thing I said to her that day as she processed loss and her sense of hopelessness was that there would come a time when she would be ready to start making a new good life for herself. When she arrived home after our appointment, she found a card from a trusted friend whom she had known since girlhood and who she knew had only her best interests at heart. The card said, *"Welcome to your brand-new life!"* It included a personal note from her friend acknowledging her loss but reminding her that she was loved and valued and that she deserved to be happy.

Sandi said, "I know most people would call that a coincidence; usually I would, but that day I understood it was more than that. Two people who care about me but who had no connection to each other said the same thing on the same day, and it was what I needed to hear. That's more than coincidence—it was a message, from somewhere, that it was time for me to move on and that I would be happy again. I decided to believe it."

Life is crowded with these little moments—coincidence, synchronicity, convergences—that have no obvious logical explanation. Usually we ignore them or fail to notice them at all. Sometimes we make meaning from them and feel silly for doing so—we don't dare tell anyone; they'd laugh at us. But, I wonder, what if, what if it was true? What if these events were indeed the operation of some force that we don't understand and can't see that wants the best for us and is arranging things precisely in the way that will be most helpful to us? What if, like Sandi, we just pretend that's the case and take a moment's hope from them? What if we say yes to the universe? Yes, I'll accept this gift and use it to guide my journey.

We might be wrong, but we might be right. After all, there's so much we don't know and can't know. Why not choose to believe that hopeful, helpful thing? In a life filled with uncertainty, as all lives are, it's good to have a bit of faith that things might work out fine and that maybe, just maybe, you don't travel alone.

The important thing is not to stop questioning. Curiosity has its own reason for existence. One cannot help but be in awe when he contemplates the mysteries of eternity, of life, of the marvelous structure of reality. It is enough if one tries merely to comprehend a little of this mystery every day.

—Albert Einstein, German-born theoretical physicist

39

THE KINDNESS
OF STRANGERS

I have always depended on the kindness of strangers.
—Tennessee Williams, American playwright

For many years I wanted to travel to Croatia. The photos and descriptions I saw were compelling, and people who had been there said the coastline was incredible and that the towns and food were like Italy thirty years ago, that is, delectable. Finally, in 2008, we decided to realize that dream. I worked for months to make the best possible itinerary for a couple traveling on their own to see as much as possible of this part of the world.

The plans called for the visit to begin in Split, ramble along the Dalmatian Coast, and end in Dubrovnik, followed by a jaunt over into Montenegro and then on to Brussels in Belgium before returning home.

Split is a town on the Dalmatian Coast built around and within the ancient walls of the Roman emperor Diocletian's palatial retirement home, which was completed in 305 CE. I had booked a room in a small hotel within the walls; indeed, we found that one of the walls of our room was the city wall itself! We were completely charmed. Our first day there, exhausted from a four-leg journey—Jacksonville to Atlanta to Brussels to Zagreb to Split—we checked in to the hotel and strolled around within the city walls, taking the measure of the place. We found it much to our liking. Ancient buildings, cobbled streets, tiny little shops and cafes tucked into the walls with living accommodations above, and flower and fruit vendors every-where. Our first meal was simple, from a patio café with six tables, and exactly what we hoped for—pasta, fresh-baked bread, and salad. Heaven. We slept well next to Diocletian's wall and thought we had made a fine decision to come to Croatia.

One of Split's advantages for a traveler is that it is the departure point for many of the ferries that serve the outlying islands that dot the Adriatic Sea. So, on our second day, we decided to take the ferry to Hvar, formerly an important trade and military base, today a popular tourist and glitterati destination. We landed in the port town of Stari Grad and set out to see the sights. Once more, we were totally charmed and enjoyed exploring on foot the town and the hills surrounding it. The weather in this part of Croatia is generally mild, and it was a beautiful day. As the time approached to make our way back to the ferry, we walked across the main square toward the cathedral. I stepped off a curb, my foot slipped, I fell, and I heard my ankle break. It didn't hurt really badly, but I thought it might be a mistake to try to walk—I knew that it was broken, even though I had never broken a bone before, because I heard it break—so my husband went in search of assistance.

So here I am, lying on the cobbled street in the hot afternoon sun, waiting for help to arrive. People stopped. One woman held an umbrella over my head; another offered me water. A few people walked on by, ignoring my plight. After a bit, my husband returned with a pharmacist he had found who spoke no English but managed to convey that she would get a taxi to take us to the doctor. Of course, the street where I fell was pedestrian only, so we had to walk a few blocks to get to the taxi, but with the help of Mark and the pharmacist, I managed to get to the taxi without using the injured foot.

Off we sped in the taxi, up the mountain to a small village, where we stopped in front of what appeared to be a small house. Inside I was taken to a room with a standard physician's office look, if one from an earlier era—maybe the 1950s or '60s. There was an examination table, and someone helped me up. In a minute or so, a man came over, dressed in slacks and an untucked shirt, with a cigarette dangling from his lip. He took my foot in one hand, my calf in the other, and yanked. I heard that bone again! But oddly, the pain stopped. He muttered, "Don't walk," and left us there. Someone took some money from my husband, and we got back into the taxi and went in search of crutches, still hoping to make the ferry. After buying what people said were the only crutches on the island, we did manage to catch the last ferry back to Split, where we headed for the emergency room at the only hospital in town.

Once there, someone took me for X-rays, and after a while, someone else came and got us and took us into a small office, where the doctor, my husband, and I looked at the X-ray and jointly determined that the fibula was fractured just above its junction with the ankle joint. So the doctor, who did speak English, said I would need a cast and sent me back out to wait. The waiting room was crowded, and a nurse was suturing a large, bleeding wound on the face of the man in the chair next to me. I leaned the other way as far as I could and hoped for the best. Finally another man came out and took me into a huge room with several beds and shelves full of supplies of one sort or another. Three or four of the other beds were also occupied, and we were all there for the same reason: the application of plaster of Paris casts to our broken limbs. Apparently bone-breaking is a common activity in Split. Cast-making takes a while, but eventually I was all encased from my foot to the knee, and they told me I could go, but I should avoid putting weight on the leg. Fortunately I had my crutches, and I left, exhausted and more than ready to make my way back to the hotel and my bed.

What I failed to anticipate was the difficulty of walking on cobbled streets with crutches I had never used before and the fact that my hotel was several blocks within the pedestrian-only sector of Split. Nor did I anticipate that my hotel room was on the third floor of a building with no elevator. I can't recall now just how Mark and I made it to the hotel; I only remember standing on the street at one point thinking, *I can't do this; I'll just have to sit here until something happens.* I do recall my horror when we got to the hotel, and I looked up the stairs and knew that I was really and truly stuck where I was. But then, before I even realized just what was happening, I was being carried up the stairs in the arms of a very large and very strong stranger, who waited at the top until Mark arrived with the key and then hurried off again. Mark said the helpful stranger worked for the hotel, but I never saw him again.

Relieved to be able to go to bed and get some rest, I didn't allow myself to think about what would happen next. My husband is an incredibly resourceful person, so I knew I could count on him to solve many of our newly acquired problems (for example, what to eat and how to get me to the next place). It seemed clear that I would not be able to continue going out and about in Split with the problem of the cobbled streets / crutches dilemma as well as the stairs. So, after a breakfast that Mark collected from the kitchen downstairs, we talked about what to do next. With regret, we decided that we ought to return home or at least make our way to Brussels, since we weren't completely confident of the diagnosis or treatment I had received so far. Mark left to make the necessary phone calls for flight arrangements, and I settled in to read a book in bed.

Later that day, Mark returned to let me know that he had been able to make changes to our flights, but that the earliest we could get a flight out of Split was three days hence. However, he said, we would be moving from our third-floor room. One of the employees of the hotel had invited us to come and stay in her parents' guesthouse, which was ground level, and I would be able to move about more freely. The hotel was happy to cancel the rest of our reservation with no charge, and someone would be up shortly to help me pack.

I accomplished the trip down the stairs on my behind, bumping down one step at a time, embarrassing but uneventful. The hotel employee, a young woman named Ana, was waiting downstairs with her father, Ivano, who had come to give us a ride in his car. I'm not sure how, but he had managed to pull the car up to the side of the hotel, and everyone helped me out and into the car and off we went.

The home he took us to was located a few minutes from the hotel on a lovely residential street just outside the walls of town. Our apartment was tucked behind the house and adjoining the grapevine-covered courtyard. Maya, Ana's mother, brought me coffee and snacks, and we sat together in the courtyard and chatted—her English was limited but far superior to my nonexistent Croatian—while Mark and Ivano went to the family's favorite restaurant and picked up Croatian comfort food for our dinner.

We stayed with them for three days. They brought us food, invited friends over for a party, and in every way, made us feel welcome and cared for. Their kindness turned my accident from disaster to delight. My trip to Croatia remains one of my happiest travel memories, even though I didn't in the end see very much of the country itself. What I saw instead was how the kindness of strangers can make brokenness into blessing. This old-fashioned, unadorned kindness is itself a kind of grace, and I've found, to my ongoing surprise, that it turns up all the time at home and abroad, unexpected, unearned, and right on time.

And a footnote—the closed reduction of my broken fibula performed by the Hvar island doctor was, in my local orthopedic surgeon's words, "perfect, just perfect," although he did remove the plaster of Paris cast and fit me out with a boot for the rest of my healing.

Three things in human life are important: the first is to be kind; the second is to be kind; and the third is to be kind.

—Henry James, American-born British writer

40

KEEP IT HOLY

I would not interfere with any creed of yours, nor want to
appear that I have all the cures. There is so much to know . . .
So many things are true . . . The way my feet must go may not
be best for you. And so I give this spark of what is light to me,
to guide you through the dark, but not tell you what to see.

—Anonymous. Found on many Reiki teachers' and
other new age healers' sites, always listed as Anon.

Kathleen and her husband, Andrew, retired and bought their
dream house in a coastal town when they were sixty-two years old.
Both had left careers in the public sector, she as a teacher and Andrew
as an engineer for the federal government. Their pensions were good,
and they had been diligent in saving for retirement and arranging
for health care. Neither of them smoked or drank to excess; they
exercised, did all their regular medical checkups, and watched their
weight.

Their new home was in an area of the country that was new to
them. They had no family or friends nearby. But Andrew had served
there briefly on a job assignment and fell in love with the climate
and the laid-back lifestyle. They weren't worried about making connections since they both made friends easily, and after all, they had
moved frequently over the years for Andrew's job. It didn't matter
much anyway because they had each other, and they were everything
to each other.

Theirs was a storybook love. Andrew doted on Kathleen, and she
thought the sun rose and set with him. They were friends, lovers, and
allies in any of life's challenges. So they began their new life with
enthusiasm and joy that they would now have more time to spend
together and to travel and to try new activities.

A few months after the move, Kathleen noticed that Andrew had become forgetful, that he often repeated himself or failed to do something he had promised to do. At first, they both ignored these instances or joked about them, but when it persisted, they took the terrifying step of having him tested for memory problems. By the end of that year, he had been diagnosed with Alzheimer's. They were both devastated. It was as if the very foundation of the world had dropped away.

As the shock began to subside, each of them did what we all do in the face of adversity: they moved into their own normal coping style. Andrew began to act as if nothing was wrong. No, he didn't deny the truth of the diagnosis, but he thought it would progress slowly and maybe never be really bad for him. Kathleen went into full battle mode. The warrior in her would find a way to save him.

And fight she did. She enrolled him in the best memory care programs in the country and in every drug trial she could find. She simply wouldn't take no for an answer from the medical people, and Andrew went along with no complaint for her sake. She became expert in dementia research and in navigating the myriad bureaucratic snarls of getting access to care. She made friends with the right people, showed up for every interview and assessment, and was never afraid to make one more phone call or ask one more person for any little scrap of help she heard about.

Alzheimer's is a formidable foe. Indeed, no matter how brave the warrior or fierce the battle, eventually it wins. And slowly, Kathleen began to recognize her defeat. She was losing her beloved to that horrible disease. The warrior left, and she became a lost and terrified little girl. Depression claimed her, and she had used up all her fighting energy in the battle against Andrew's illness. She collapsed. Although she continued to care for Andrew and to develop as best she could a team and resources to assure his care, she stopped taking care of herself. She didn't sleep much or well, she gained weight, she stopped exercising, and she began to close herself off from the world.

The promise of their new home was now a trap that bound her to isolation and loneliness. So far from family and established friends, she felt cut off from help or comfort, and as Andrew's disease created an ever-widening space between the two of them, all alone.

As part of the support system Kathleen created for herself, I heard this story as it was evolving. Each session I watched her grieve and grieved with her and wanted so badly to relieve her pain. I know that she valued our time together, because she said it allowed her to freely express things she felt she couldn't say to Andrew or to most of the people she encountered. She said that she needed to know she had a place to be as sad as she needed to be or as angry, because "People can't take it. They try to make me feel better or try to tell me to feel some other way, or they avoid me. Most people just avoid me. They don't want to be touched by this disease." She liked that I offered no platitudes, but rather said in various ways, "It hurts so badly because it matters so much to you."

Part of the cruelty of Alzheimer's is its slow/fast progression. On the one hand, a person can be sick with it for years and years, taking an exorbitant toll on the caregivers in terms of basic things like money, energy, and time, as well as the excruciating pain of watching someone you love melt away. On the other hand, the progression of the disease is always too fast because it is terminal, and the end is always too soon.

Kathleen walked through it. She fought it, she accepted it, she fought it again, she mourned, she gave up and then got up and did what needed doing all over again. The walk was long and arduous, and she often despaired that she would make it through and despaired as well for what might lie on the other side.

One day she came in and told me this story.

Over the past weekend, Andrew had become violent and ultimately had to be hospitalized for his own and others' safety. Kathleen said it broke her heart to see him in so much pain and confusion, inconsolable, and then broke it again to leave him in the facility. Back at home, late at night, exhausted and at her wit's end, she fell on the bed in the quiet house, and then, as she tells it, "Quietness said, 'Be still, be calm, all will be well.'" This was a real voice, she said, not one in her head, so she asked, "Who said that?" aloud, and the answer was, "Know that I am near."

She said that she felt "still and enveloped," and shortly after fell asleep for the best sleep in years. When she awoke, the calmness and security was still with her, as, she said, it was on the day we spoke. She didn't understand it, nor have any theories about what had happened. She simply knew that it was real and that she was not alone.

Kathleen had grown up in a Catholic family, but moved away from the church gradually in adulthood. Soon after Andrew's diagnosis, she returned to the church, hoping to find answers or consolation there. She loved the ritual, but didn't stay because she was infuriated when people said she should accept "God's will." She said she absolutely refused to believe this dreadful disease was God's will, and if it was, she wanted no part of that God or the people who claimed they spoke for him.

So the voice, she said, may have been God or may have been something she knew nothing about. Its origins were a mystery, but, she said, that was okay with her, because she knew that whatever it was or wherever it came from, it was real, it had power, and what she heard was true. She knew that she was not alone.

Over the weeks and months that followed, she continued to deal with the demands of caregiving and she continued to grieve, but something had changed. Her profound loneliness slipped away and, with it, the desperation she had carried in her body and her soul throughout Andrew's illness. She began to plan for her own future and to make clear and discerning choices about her own healing. She stopped listening to voices that failed to nurture and reached out to those that did. She started to look like someone who was cared for.

She said she told only me and one of the hospice workers about this experience. She didn't want to trust it to the hands of those who might discount it or try to explain it to her. She thought it was too precious to be handled uncaringly and that she needed it to remain holy and wholly mysterious in order to be able to draw its strength.

I respected her desire not to give it a name. So often, we make things smaller than they are with the names we give them, from our need to claim and control them. Still, privately and with my own understandings of it, I call it grace. Like Kathleen, I don't need to understand it or know its origins. I only need to pay attention when it calls and accept its offer. And as best I can, keep it holy.

I can tell you that it takes great strength to surrender. You have to know that you are not going to collapse. Instead, you are going to open to a power that you don't even know, and it is going to come to meet you. In the process of healing, this is one of the huge things that I have discovered. People recognized the energy coming to meet them. When they opened to another energy, a love, a divine love, came through to meet them. That is what is known as grace. We all sing about amazing grace. It is a gift. I think that it comes through the work that we do. For some people, it can come out of the blue, but I know that in my own situation, the grace came through incredible vigilance.

—Marion Woodman, Canadian author and Jungian analyst

41

SAVING GRACE

A colleague who was seeing Bethany's mother and felt it would be inappropriate to see two members of the same family, especially since her client viewed Bethany as the sole and singular source of all her problems, referred Bethany to me. I accepted the referral and then wondered what I had gotten myself into.

When finally we met at her first appointment, I was surprised. She was a neatly dressed, rather ordinary-looking woman of about forty, with excellent manners and educated speech. She provided a highly coherent history and expressed a willingness to work in therapy. She also admitted that she had an addiction to cocaine that had endured more than fifteen years and that she had five previous failed attempts at psychotherapy and treatment for her addiction. She said that she had once been given a diagnosis of bipolar disorder by a psychiatrist at one of the treatment facilities, but the medications he prescribed made her sick and didn't seem to prevent her from going back to cocaine.

She herself believed that some of her problems were the result of family dynamics rather than her own illness. She had learned about the structure of the dysfunctional family in one of her treatment experiences and said that she saw herself as the inevitable product of her "alcoholic" family, not that anyone now living drank problematically, but her paternal grandfather was probably alcoholic, and the legacy of his addiction carried forward, creating a family structure determined more from denial and avoidance than love and authenticity.

This woman is smart, I said to myself, *maybe too smart for her own good.*

Gradually over the weeks of our sessions, I learned more about this dysfunctional family—her theory was in fact fairly accurate—and even more about my client's ability to use her good mind to shape a story that served to reinforce her disease process and block any movement toward change. Cocaine addiction, like all drug addictions, is a deadly disease and ultimately leads to total destruction of the personality; it usually costs the addict his or her livelihood, family, and everything of value, including life itself. Bethany had escaped many of the more obvious and devastating consequences because her father regularly rescued her. He provided financial support and the help of medical and legal professionals when required, facilitated conflicts with employers or landlords or others as needed, and generally stood between Bethany and whatever negative outcomes her cocaine use created.

She understood this as well as I did, and thought he ought to stop for his own sake, the sake of the rest of the family, and maybe even for hers, but she admitted that she would probably ask for his help the next time something bad happened. She told me she wanted to give up the cocaine and had been able to at times for weeks or even months, but that there would always come a moment when she remembered what it felt like to be high and nothing would stop her from going back there. She said she would lie, steal, take risks, shirk all of her responsibilities, and abandon all her dreams to get that feeling again.

I thought it meant something that she was honest with me about it, and I hoped it meant that together we might discover an opening for change. I had no idea where that opening might be, but I was willing to stay present and listen carefully and work hard to help her uncover her truth.

Addictions of all kinds are magnificent liars. They tell their host that they are the way and the light and that life will be meaningless without them. They say that they represent truth and beauty and comfort and power and that nothing else can compare. Because of the way that the drugs or the process affect the cells of the brain, these lies become true in one way, and this effect robs the addict of the power of choice, along with the ability to love, to feel joy, or to grow and evolve into a truer, deeper, more authentic person.

Bethany, in her years of service to her drug of choice, had begun to believe all those lies. She no longer knew the truth that she was lovable and capable of loving, that joy was possible for her, or that there was so much self she had yet to discover. She just didn't know this. And in not knowing or believing or trusting, she kept returning to the only source of good things that she now knew. She was completely captive to cocaine's lies.

As a therapist, I have seen this story a thousand times or more. Every addict, whether the addiction is to drugs, alcohol, sex, food, or pride and a false self-image, is truly imprisoned by the process. Addiction locks the door and bars the windows and turns off the light. There is literally no way out.

Which turns out to mean that something outside the addict has to find a way in. We therapists hope we can find that something—a word, an intervention, or a suggestion that will create the possibility of change. Many people devote themselves heartily and with all goodwill and ethical force to this hope. Sometimes it works. Most times it doesn't. Consequences sometimes knock down the walls that addiction built, and the addict peeks through the destruction and sees some tiny bit of light that pulls him forward. When that happens, it's good if someone is there to help and to guide and to accompany him through the rubble.

But most of the time, recovery begins because of the action of grace. The addict suddenly sees what he or she could not see before.

From somewhere unknown and apparently without cause, the veil is lifted, the door opens, and the addict is now able to do what she could not do before. She is somehow given a glimpse of the higher truth and can see addiction's lies for what they are.

This happened for Bethany in the county jail. About a year after I began seeing her, she was caught shoplifting. I can't say why, but she refused her father's offer of help and chose to accept her consequences. This was not her first arrest, but it was the first time she actually went to court. All the other times, her father had arranged through attorneys or through his own connections to get the charges dropped. This time, she said, "No, I'll go to court."

She was found guilty and sentenced to make restitution and to one year's probation, but, the judge said, she ought to spend a few days in jail so she would understand what any future offense might hold for her. She told me later that she was terrified and thought she had made an awful mistake not accepting her father's help. She didn't think she could survive even a few nights in jail (her sentence demanded five nights and days). But she stayed away from cocaine and presented herself as ordered on the appointed day and was duly locked away.

She said she expected horrible people who would mock her and perhaps harm her, but that most of the women were kind to her and tried to help with her adjustment, although some of them did laugh at her fear. A picky eater who was used to nice things, she found the physical circumstances of jail were hard for her—the food plain and unappetizing, the blanket rough, the mattress hard, the walls an ugly shade of green. She hated the sound of the intercom and the clang when doors were opened and closed. They never turned the lights out, which she hated and yet was glad for because it helped with her fear.

On her third night in jail, when she was trying unsuccessfully to sleep, she said she was suddenly aware of someone above her, floating near the ceiling, who said, "You never have to use drugs again, and if you don't, I promise you I will be with you, and you will have a good life, better than you can now imagine." The image disappeared as suddenly as it arrived. Bethany said she was frightened and confused, but that she knew it did not come from inside herself, that it was neither hallucination nor dream. She didn't know what it was or where it came from, but it wasn't fiction or imagination. It was true.

By the time I saw her and heard this story, she had survived her time in jail, and she was back home and back at work. She told me about it timidly and asked me if I planned to have her committed, if I thought she was crazy, or if I thought it might be real.

There are professional and technical things I could tell you about the discrimination I made before answering her question, but you and I would both be bored by them, so I'll just include what I actually said, which was, "I think the most important thing is what you do with that experience."

She agreed. Here's what she did. That was more than fifteen years ago, and she's never used cocaine again. She has established a career, made amends with her family, and is now a valued and valuable part of family and community. She didn't do that alone. She had help from her family, from me, from a support group, and after a while, a church that she found and became part of.

But it was grace that saved her.

God's grace is not defined as God being forgiving to us even though we sin. Grace is when God is a source of wholeness, which makes up for my failings. My failings hurt me and others and even the planet, and God's grace to me is that my brokenness is not the final word . . . it's that God makes beautiful things out of even my own shit. Grace isn't about God creating humans and flawed beings and then acting all hurt when we inevitably fail and then stepping in like the hero to grant us grace—like saying, "Oh, it's OK, I'll be the good guy and forgive you." It's God saying, "I love the world too much to let your sin define you and be the final word. I am a God who makes all things new."

—Nadia Bolz-Weber, Lutheran minister and author

42

GRACIOUS!

Be like the sun for grace and mercy. Be like the night to
cover others' faults. Be like running water for generosity.
Be like death for rage and anger. Be like the Earth for
modesty. Appear as you are. Be as you appear.

—Rumi, thirteenth-century Persian poet, Islamic scholar, and Sufi mystic

We have an expression in the South. When something surprising happens, good or bad, people often say, "Gracious!" Or if they are a little older, "Gracious me!" The Cambridge Dictionary tells me that this expression is used to express how surprised, shocked, angry, or frustrated you are and that it hails from England and probably dates back to the 1700s. The first recorded reference I can find is attributed to Charles Dickens.

The online *Urban Dictionary* says that sweet little old ladies frequently use this expression in the South as a "minced oath," a substitute for cursing. Well, yes, another act of graciousness. What some modern people call honesty or authenticity could more properly be called vulgarity or rudeness. There is nothing wrong with treating people with consideration and kindness. A gentle touch does no harm.

We have a friend, a lovely woman in her fifties, who embodies graciousness. I watch her with a kind of wonder and fascination, hoping to learn her secret. Everyone feels better after an encounter with Ann. You can see in their faces what I feel around her—accepted and respected and that I matter.

Ann and I are on a committee together. As it often is with committees, this one can get contentious. People disagree, sometimes heatedly, and every so often, disagreement turns to criticism, even personal attack. Ann never offends. She manages to express her thoughts and opinions, but unerringly in a manner that holds out respect for you and your no-matter-how-different opinion. She does all this without ever seeming to be trying to do it. It appears effortless, as if it just comes naturally to her. I don't know if it does, or if she worked at it at some point in her life. Perhaps she learned it from a parent or family member; perhaps she had a role model that she emulated out in the world someplace. Or maybe it does come naturally to her from somewhere in her unique genetic code.

But I have to believe that I could learn to be like her or at least more like her if I tried. My dearest wish is that I leave the people I encounter feeling better about themselves and about this world we live in. I get impatient with myself when I fall short of that, when I let my own impatience, fatigue, or self-importance control my interactions with others. That's not the person I want to be—I want to be more like Ann.

This desire to be better than I am doesn't mean that I have abandoned my commitment to be a friend to myself. It doesn't mean I don't love myself. It does mean that I am honest about myself in this way and that I see something I want to follow and grow toward. It means that I am still on the journey, and I've seen a sign that points the way in the direction I need to travel. It doesn't make Ann better than me; it makes her my teacher.

So far, here's what I've learned. Ann is genuinely interested in other people. She is polite, and she is kind. She doesn't seem to be overly concerned with herself, but neither does she seem self-neglectful. She takes good care of herself. She often says no to requests, but with just the right combination of words and expression that people still feel good about asking. She is available, but not intrusive. She is genuine and generous.

I don't know if I'll be able to be as gracious as she is. I am opinionated, outspoken, and sometimes self-absorbed. I have a wicked sense of humor that I enjoy but sometimes leaves others feeling a little uncomfortable. I don't mean the kind of humor that is demeaning, just a tendency not to take things too seriously. I mean no harm, but my mouth just opens, the words come out, and there you are. I know these things about myself and they are okay with me, but still, I'd love to learn some of Ann's graciousness.

There's a principle in psychology called projection, the idea that we recognize our own previously unacknowledged or undeveloped traits, both good and bad, in people around us and then react to the person and treat them as if the traits were theirs, not ours. It is lovely to imagine that I am able to recognize this quality in Ann because I have it within myself, that I only have to remove the barriers of unconsciousness and the wounds that confine it for it to emerge. That might be true, and it might also be true that I simply didn't learn it. But either way, I am convinced that with effort and a little help, I can learn to be more gracious. And I am equally convinced that when I begin to do the work, the help will come. That's grace, waiting patiently for me to begin. Even now, when I've come to know that I can count on grace, I will be surprised because it seems to be in the nature of grace to show itself in unexpected ways and at unanticipated times.

Maybe in the end, that's why we say, " *Good gracious!*"

And grace, which is the flowing, creative activity, of love itself, is what makes all goodness possible.

—Gerald May, American psychiatrist and author

43

THE COLORS OF LIGHT

Gratitude bestows reverence, allowing us to encounter everyday epiphanies, those transcendent moments of awe that change forever how we experience life and the world.

—John Milton, seventeenth-century English author and poet

The light in the South of France is different from the light everywhere else in the world, just like the light on the desert in Egypt is a color that exists no place else on earth. Most evenings I watch the light change over the pond behind my house, and all the familiar things out there become other things as they accept the colors that are the gift of the changing light. It seems to me that every place I've been has its own distinct and specific light, and I am in awe of that.

I don't know what it means.

I think, though, that it has meaning and that it is imperative that I continue trying to understand. Since I have seen the light and noticed its variety, it must be my task to do something with that, to make meaning of it, to know the whys and wherefores of it so that I am made whole by it. The gift of awe, when received, carries an obligation—an obligation of care.

Awe is the emotion that combines reverence, respect, dread, and wonder and is usually inspired by either great authority, genius, beauty, might, or the sublime. We feel awe when we experience through our senses an object or event or individual that appears to be far superior to us in power or magnitude or understanding, when we are humbled by the size of a thing or by its nature. It's when I am confronted with magnificence and I know that I could not do that, make that, create that, that I feel awe. I have felt awe at the sight of a painting, the sound of a symphony, or the words in a book. I have felt awe on hearing stories of bravery or personal sacrifice in service of others or a cause, but more often, it is in nature that the feeling is aroused within me. I see the light in France, and I wonder, how can this happen? How can the light here be so beautiful and so different from the light in other places? What does it even mean to say that the light is different? But it is; I see the difference and I trust it, and it is completely beyond my understanding.

There's a part of my mind right now saying, "Well, yes, but science, someone more scientifically knowledgeable, would understand, would be able to explain the light." And that is probably true, but I'm willing to wager than even that smart person would not be able to explain scientifically the power of the light—the way that light makes me feel in the heart, in the belly, in my head, in the very cells of my body. That's between the light and me, and we're not telling. It's personal. It's holy.

It's grace.

I don't let anybody take my awe from me. I protect it like the treasure it is. I don't talk about it with anybody I don't completely trust to honor it. I don't listen to explanations that reduce it to formulas or equations. I don't permit platitudes.

And I don't use the word "awesome" in ordinary conversation except with irony when I'm thoroughly annoyed with exaggerations of one kind or another, and when I do that, it feels like blasphemy. Awe is not to be taken lightly. If God wants to talk to me in that language, I want to listen. With awe. And gratitude.

I don't think that faith, whatever you're being faithful about, really can be scientifically explained. And I don't want to explain this whole life business through truth, science. There's so much mystery. There's so much awe.

—Jane Goodall, British primatologist and anthropologist

44

SAVING GRACES

All of the following meet the definitional standard of grace, in that they aren't earned or merited. They simply are and sometimes come our way. We must practice noticing and appreciating them.

- Laughter
- A hand to hold
- Flowers
- Sunshine
- Rain
- A child's delight
- A good cry
- Support from a friend
- A casserole
- Clean sheets and a good pillow
- "Thank you."
- "You are welcome."
- Stars in the sky
- An unexpected boon
- A surprise
- Respect
- A compliment
- Music
- A card, letter, e-mail saying, "I care"
- Rainbows
- Soft pj's
- A hug
- A hot shower
- A parent's love
- A child's love
- Oceans
- Dandelions
- Gratitude
- Dogs and cats
- Courtesy
- Patience

- Courage
- Good coffee
- Or tea
- Art
- Charity
- Beauty
- Nature
- Warmth
- Smiling faces
- Kindness

45

Now and then it's good to pause in our pursuit
of happiness and just be happy.

—Guillaume Apollinaire, early twentieth-century French poet

Franklin created quite a stir when he came for his first visit with me and continued to do so at every appointment. He was a large, outgoing man with a loud voice, and he chatted with whomever was in the waiting room and developed quite a noisy friendship with the front-office staff. He sincerely wanted to know how everyone was and wanted to share his own news with them as well. Everything about him was inappropriate for a therapy office. He was too loud, too personal, too upbeat, too large, and he violated all the unspoken rules about therapy office waiting room demeanor—be quiet, be serious, avoid eye contact, maybe even look a little sad if you can. He walked right in being himself—boisterous, happy, and engaged—completely unaware that there was anything out of order about that.

He had been referred following an automobile accident that left him with an acutely painful spinal injury. He described this as "outrageously unfair" since he had broken his back thirty years earlier and had been disabled ever since. For all those years, he had been in pain until about a year prior, when he found a pain management physician who was able to find the right combination of medications to control the pain. Franklin had been pain free for one year out of the past thirty until the accident, and now he was in pain again and the doctor told him he would not be able to add any medication or to change the medication without risking either overdose or a resumption of the chronic pain condition. This news, he said, had initially been devastating, the thought of going back to a life of chronic pain almost more than he could bear. But the physician had suggested that he see a therapist and learn some behavioral pain management techniques, as well as assess the level of his depression. And so he came to me.

I can say with all honesty, I had never met a less depressed person. The man I met that day was full of joy. I was eager to hear his story. Franklin was happy to tell me, and so we began.

He grew up in a large working-class family with problems like most families. His mother was a cold woman, who did her job as caregiver for the family, but with resentment and complaint her daily refrain. Nothing anyone did pleased her, and she grumbled that there wasn't enough money, that her family neglected her and their responsibilities, that their house was too small and too shabby, and that her husband was a failure as a man. Her children were ungrateful, lazy, and too stupid to accomplish anything in life. According to Franklin, she cooked, she cleaned, and she criticized.

His father, not surprisingly, was seldom home. Franklin thought he was a good, hard-working man who treated his children and wife kindly, but he worked long hours and spent a good bit of time in the neighborhood taverns. Franklin didn't think he had a drinking problem. He just didn't want to come home, and that's what men in his peer group did. They met at taverns and drank and talked and went home for meals and sleep and on holidays and for family emergencies.

Franklin left home at eighteen, married at nineteen, and got a job working for the railroad. He said he was happy; he loved his wife, and he was glad to be working and providing for his family. They had two children, and that added to his happiness. Unlike his father, he stayed away from taverns—he said he loved being a husband and father.

When he fell off the top of a railcar and broke his back, they told him he would never walk again, and because it was a union job with good insurance, he was granted full disability. He said the pain was horrible and that there were many days he considered suicide, but his love for his family kept him going and kept him trying to walk again. Eventually, with lots of help from medical personnel and physical therapy and, I imagine, sheer determination, he was able to walk and to return to some of the activities he had enjoyed before his injury. He loved to cook and grow vegetables, and he could do that again, though not without pain. The pain was constant, with peaks and valleys, but never completely gone until he found this new physician who discovered the magic formula for providing pain relief without sedation. And then came the car accident.

Franklin said at first it took him back to the early days following his first major back injury. He considered giving up. He said he raged at the hospital staff and wanted to find the driver who had hit him and beat him to a pulp. And, he said, he cried, long and loud and without consolation. He despaired.

And then, he said, he woke up one morning in the hospital and said to himself, "I've done this before—I can do it again," and called me to make the appointment. He told his wife to bring him his favorite food and a chocolate cake.

I saw him for ten sessions. During that time, we worked together to help him discover ways to manage the pain of his injury. He said it was helpful, but he said what he liked most about coming in was having someone *to talk about feelings with*. He said that the people in his life didn't do that very often, and he was glad to have that chance. On the anniversary of his father's death, he sat across from me and cried and talked about how much he missed him and wished they could have had more time together.

When his mentally ill daughter refused to let him see his granddaughter, the love of his life, he cried again, and when she changed her mind, he came in all smiles and told me stories about the time he spent with the little girl and with her mother and his plans for providing for them upon his death.

Because, you see, throughout this brief period, Franklin was also dealing with a cancer diagnosis that was bound to be terminal. He didn't know if he had six months or six years, but he knew his death was near. He was sick a good bit and had three hospitalizations and two surgeries, but he didn't stop working on managing his pain so that he could live fully now.

So that he could hold on to the joy that was his birthright. He knew what so many of us have forgotten or never knew—that joy is always now. It isn't waiting out there somewhere, nor is it stuck somewhere in the past. It's right now, this minute, this day, no matter what else is present. He said at our last session, when I asked what his plans were, "I learned after the first accident that if I'm ever going to be happy, I have to be happy now. No matter what. So that's what I plan to do—keep on being happy."

Franklin passed away not long after that. Everyone in my office was so grateful they got to know him.

Joy, rather than happiness, is the goal of life, for joy is the emotion which accompanies our fulfilling our natures as human beings. It is based on the experience of one's identity as a being of worth and dignity.

—Rollo May, American existential psychologist and author

46

JOURNEY TO SELF

What we call our destiny is truly our character and that character can be altered. The knowledge that we are responsible for our actions and attitudes does not need to be discouraging, because it also means that we are free to change this destiny. One is not in bondage to the past, which has shaped our feelings, to race, inheritance, background. All this can be altered if we have the courage to examine how it formed us. We can alter the chemistry provided we have the courage to dissect the elements.

—Anaïs Nin, American essayist and memoirist, born in France to Cuban parents

I n my office and my writing, I encourage a radical self-honesty and accountability, combined with total self-acceptance. There's a very practical reason why I do that. Nothing else works. So long as we lie to ourselves and practice self-deception in all its forms, we are lost. So long as we make excuses and wallow in self-pity and a sense of victimization, we are lost. So long as we condemn and brutalize ourselves, we are lost.

In order to be found again, to be reclaimed, to be redeemed, we must work diligently to give up our delusions and our alibis, to come fully into adulthood and accept responsibility for our lives, and we must find a way to be kind to ourselves while we're doing it. Much of our illness, corruption, and disturbance is caused by our unwillingness to face up to what is true, to own our faults and failings and attempt to correct them, and to treat ourselves with the same love and compassion we would offer our child or our dearest friend. There is no other way. Neither fancy words nor appealing formulas will fix our lives. There is no secret except the one a client of mine found and shared with me: "I've discovered there is no magic pill. I will have to do my own work if I want to heal."

Ah, how we long for the magic pill. We seek it in gurus, in medicines, in practices, in formulas, in books, and in slogans. We look to our leaders, our healers, our friends, or our families to be our solutions. Sometimes we look in darkness for the light; drugs, alcohol, sex, risk—all promise redemption. No one chooses a life of desperation; they find it at the end of a misguided search for the solution to their problem. Carl Jung, in a letter to Bill Wilson, one of the founders of Alcoholics Anonymous, expressed his idea that it is the quest for a spiritual solution that leads one to alcohol and hence to alcoholism and that the only real solution then must be a spiritual one. Regardless of how you define "spiritual," I think the same is true for all types of human suffering.

We are all on a journey to self, and that journey is by its nature a spiritual one that calls for—no, demands—honesty, integrity, and love. When we get lost, when for any reason we forget who we are and who we must try to be, we suffer. Our symptoms may take many forms—depression, anxiety, addictions, yes, but also, conceit, irritability, harshness, greed, cruelty, all the possible defects humans are prone to. All of these and others are nothing more than symptoms of our separation from self and signposts to guide the journey home.

I think this sounds more like a religious formulation than a clinical one. You might be excused for doubting my credibility here. I am no theologian or spiritual guide. I have no formal training in those subjects at all, nor can I lay any claim to exceptional personal religious experience. My insights come entirely from my own explorations and from my observations of others' journeys from the vantage point of the therapist's chair. We, my clients and I, have all eventually come to the point when we had to give up any hope of the easy fix and sign on to the hard work of healing.

Rhonda came to my office for the first time when she was fifty-two and worried about getting old. She told me she had looked in the mirror the week before, and "I saw my mother and I was terrified." As the story unfolded, it seemed she was terrified of many things. She had recently begun to obsess about tornadoes and other natural disasters, as well as worrying to the point of tears whenever her husband left the house. She had retired early and was at home most of the time now and indeed had begun to fear leaving the house. None of these fears were familiar to her. Until recently, she had worked full-time, helped care for her aging, now deceased parents, and enjoyed outdoor activities, including camping with her husband and her real passion, long-distance cycling. She said that she still cycled, but only recreationally, and that she'd lost interest in camping.

This was to be her third attempt at psychotherapy. The first therapist was a woman she saw for about a year when she was in her twenties. She said that the therapy helped with what she described as depression that she believed was connected to problems from her childhood. She said her mother had been both critical and neglectful and that she had accepted her mother's treatment of her as a reflection of her own value and worth. She felt that the therapy had helped her see herself more clearly and to begin to heal from those childhood wounds. The second therapy had taken place about ten years before our time together and was initiated by a return of the depression, which during the course of therapy had worsened until she became suicidal and, in her words, "totally crazy. I cried all the time; I blamed my husband and fought with him. I couldn't sleep or eat, and I began having hallucinations. I thought my father had molested me, and the therapist and Bill [her husband] both told me I was wrong, that it didn't happen, but I was sure of it, and I was so ashamed, I wanted to die."

She said that she was given medication and increased the frequency of her therapy appointments and that eventually she got better. She denied any suicide attempts, but remembered that time as the worst of her life. She and Bill had regained their equilibrium as a couple in most ways, except, she said, that Bill no longer regarded her as the strong one in their marriage as he had until this happened. "He doesn't trust me anymore."

I wondered aloud what she now believed about the possible sexual abuse, whether she thought this was something that had happened in the past or that she had indeed hallucinated those experiences. She said she honestly didn't know, that she only recalled, or thought she recalled, images of hands on her body, and a sort of complicated mélange of feelings and impressions associated with bedtime and her father. I asked her if it was important to her to have an answer to this, and she said, "No, not now; I don't want to go crazy again. And I don't want to have to deal with Bill's reaction if that came up again."

So, we began where she was, with her current anxieties and with her fear of growing old, of becoming her mother. Her symptoms were the signposts we used to lead us on her journey to self. Over the time we spent together, she learned a great deal about herself that she hadn't known before. She learned that she was strong and capable and creative and kind. She learned that she had missed out on a lot because she had defined herself too narrowly. Believing that she was not quite good enough to be loved for herself, she had tried hard to please others, even when it meant ignoring her own needs or even violating her own values. One day, after reading a book that she initially saw as "too hard," she proudly announced that she had understood what she read and even wished she had people to talk to about the book's content. She told me, "I didn't learn anything at school. I was too busy entertaining everyone. I didn't even know I liked learning. But I do."

She also learned that she could set limits with people and say no, that she didn't have to give herself to everyone who asked, from friends who misused her kindness, to strangers who exploited her generosity, to groups that took advantage of her competence and willingness to contribute. She could just say "No" or "I don't want to" or "Please don't talk to me that way" or, even, "Go away." She found her voice. She could say what she thought and ask for what she wanted, and she could also give praise or comfort or a creative idea. She no longer needed to please because she had learned that she couldn't rely on others to define her, that she needed to do the defining herself and please herself and hold herself accountable to her own standards and values.

Rhonda left many of the best parts of herself behind in the child who was mistreated by those who might have loved her and encouraged her growth. She failed to claim her birthright, her beauty, and her potentials because she accepted others' definition of her. She made herself smaller than she was in order to hold on to whatever slices of acceptance and approval, of belonging, that she knew how to obtain. She told herself lies about who she was, and she developed skills to help her survive. In the dark of her nights, she told herself that she was flawed and inadequate and only lovable when she did what *they* wanted. No wonder she was afraid. She knew that she could not count on herself for protection and love.

After a while, her anxiety disappeared. She didn't really notice it leaving, and one day, when I asked about her anxiety level, she met that question with what can only be described as a blank stare before she said, "Oh, yeah, that's why I came here, isn't it?"

Before she moved on from our work together, she told me that she had the answer to the question of whether she had been sexually abused as a child. She said that she knew her father molested her, that she actually remembered it vividly and that she always had. But she said she hadn't been able to tell anyone because she was afraid they would disapprove or be disgusted by it. She said that her need to be pleasing was stronger than her desire to be healed, so she kept the truth to herself even when that truth pushed to be heard. So she hinted at the facts, hoping someone would pick them up and affirm them for her. Denied, the truth pushed harder, and she and everyone else called that "going crazy." Eventually, to save herself, she found a way to push the truth back down, but she learned, as we all do, that truth won't stay down. It always finds ways to show itself, if not as itself, then as symptom or symbol that offers a clue or a glimmer of where to look next.

Occasionally Rhonda comes in for what she calls "fine-tuning" when she encounters a new challenge or sometimes to celebrate new lessons learned. Each time, she tells me how grateful she is to be living this life now, how much more she has learned, how many paths have opened for her. I don't need to be told. I can barely recognize her as the person who first walked in my office. You can see her changes in her face, in the way she walks and talks, in the clothes she wears, and in her eyes. She looks older. It's odd, isn't it, that her greatest fear—of growing old—is precisely what became her greatest gift? She grew up, and in so doing, she redeemed the past and claimed herself. She grew old enough and bold enough to tell the truth, to become accountable to herself, and to love herself through it all. It always works.

I do not mean to imply by this that a man can determine just what his world or his life will be like. A man, after all, is only a man. He stands somewhere between absolute freedom on the one hand, and total helplessness on the other. All of his important decisions must be made on the basis of insufficient data. It is enough if a man accepts his freedom, takes his best shot, does what he can, faces the consequences of his acts, and makes no excuses. It may not be fair that a man gets to have total responsibility for his own life without total control over it, but it seems to me that for good or for bad, that's just the way it is.

—Sheldon B. Kopp, American psychotherapist and author

EPILOGUE

Notre Dame Cathedral, Paris, 1997

Testament of Faith & Hope

1. I believe in the power of each effort.
2. I believe in the possibility of change.
3. I believe in doing the right thing.
4. I believe in the essential goodness of the universe despite negative evidence.
5. I believe love is always worth it.
6. I believe that each life has purpose & meaning & value.
7. I believe in miracles — unexpected, unearned blessings.
8. I believe in prayer.
9. I have faith that help is available from friends, from strangers, from God.
10. I believe in truth & honesty.
11. I believe in compassion.
12. I believe in the power of one person trying to do the right thing.

Journal Entry, 2000

MANY PATHS

There are three things extremely hard:
steel, a diamond, and to know one's self.

—Benjamin Franklin, American scientist, politician, and Founding Father

My client Rhonda and I both used psychotherapy on our journey back to self. Psychotherapy is a powerful tool that many, many people have found helpful in restoring health and achieving personal goals. When it works as it should, therapy provides the safety and structure that is necessary for healing and growth. But therapy is not the only path for self-discovery; there are many paths that can lead us back to ourselves and forward to our next best lives.

Each of us must find the path that is right for us. Some find their way through religion or nonreligious spiritual practice. Others find their way in the normal course of a life, with all its demands, defeats, and achievements. However different the paths might look from the outside, they all have common elements that permit the development of self and the restoration of the integrity of the spirit.

Perhaps a glimpse of what happens in good psychotherapy can serve to describe these common elements. Clearly, not all psychotherapy is good therapy. The tiny bits of my story highlight some ways it can be bad. There are others, some much worse. But most psychotherapy aims to be good, and in my experience, most therapists work very hard at providing the correct treatment and the proper environment for change and healing. Still, the therapist and the client exist in a larger environment that affects what happens in the therapy room. Nothing happens in isolation: we are all part of the larger whole, and it operates with or without our permission. So the therapist is trained in the dominant model of the time and sets out with best intentions to help the people he or she sees. But what if the dominant model is flawed, as it always is? What if the dominant model is hugely helpful for many people, but for one particular person, entirely without benefit? How can therapists know and adjust when they only know what they have been taught or been able to figure out so far? What if the therapist is tired or worried or injured or caught in the web of his or her own personality flaws? What if the fit just isn't good? The therapist may be a great therapist for many people, but not for you. No one's to blame—the fit just doesn't work.

Looking back, I'm so grateful and a little awed that I persisted in trying therapy when I had failed it or it had failed me in the past. I can only assume that I was both determined and desperate for a solution to my life and that, in another, less explicable sense, it was part of my destiny, a working out of my life that I was neither in charge of nor responsible for, a bit of grace and a gift from mystery.

I didn't know back then to trust the urgings of my inner self, to let them guide me consciously and with intent. I only knew that I needed help, and this was one place I might find it. I tried many other cures as well. I was always looking for something to fix me—a job, a relationship, a nose job, more education, more money, a confusing variety of religions, an array of alternative practices from astrology to meditation to psychic readings. I even followed a self-proclaimed psychic for a while, who told me I could read auras and interpret past lives if I developed my abilities. I can't and I didn't, but for a little while that helped me hold onto hope for myself.

But somehow, I kept going back to therapy and trying it again, and came at last to the right therapist for me and to a time when I was available to be helped. And I began to grow and take shape as the person I am, rather than the shell of a person I had been before in my eager attempts to make myself into the person I thought the world wanted me to be. I had been trying so hard to discover the secret, the formula that would make me acceptable and thus happy, this elusive strategy that would make my life work. Not knowing, not even dreaming, that the only secret was to find a way to be true and loyal to me, the inner me, the unknown me, the flawed and broken, and strong and good and indomitable, me. And when I began to learn that in a therapist's office, I could then reach out and strengthen and build with blocks from other worthwhile paths and with the help of other people who were walking this same way.

What helped? How do I now define good therapy and, indeed, more broadly, the necessary elements of a healing path? It begins with respect, a profound sense that the person who has presented himself or herself for guidance is unique and valuable and has ideas and values that must be included, and with the deep understanding of the sacred nature of the work to be done. Good therapy is patient and kind and encouraging and demanding and always hopeful. Good therapy waits and endures and asks and listens and shares and suggests. Good therapy accepts everything, and simultaneously only the best. Good therapy knows how weak we are and how strong. Good therapy wants the best for us. It doesn't judge, but it doesn't agree to harm. It looks a lot like love.

Therapists are people, and they all—we all—fail to do any of this perfectly all of the time. Some days we are grumpy or impatient or worried or sleepy or self-absorbed. Despite all our good training on how to keep that out of our practice, some of it creeps in from time to time. Good therapy can withstand that, too, because the process is bigger than its two participants. The process has power in and of itself. Some of the power is in the ritual, the regular time and place and duration and formalities that form the shape of the path. The ritual is the container, and the container has healing energy all on its own.

But by far, the most important reason that good therapy can tolerate the therapist's imperfections is that the therapist is the second most important person in the room. The work, the learning, the healing comes from within. It isn't given by the therapist, but welcomed and affirmed and, from time to time, safeguarded while the client journeys elsewhere.

So what can good therapy teach us about what to look for from the many pathways of self-discovery? First, it must offer respect—for yourself, for others, and for the process itself. Secondly, it must make room for everything without judgment or rejection, while simultaneously desiring the good and the valuable. It must be patient, kind, interested, involved, and active. It doesn't teach so much as offer information for learning and listen with respect to objections and questions. The path serves the pilgrim, not the other way around.

My psychic guru was, I think, a deeply sincere woman, with a loving heart and a generous spirit. She may have believed what she taught. She was, however, a woman seeking affirmation and, having found a following, guarded it jealously. I've never understood the power she had over her followers. People worked very hard to please her, and no one dared question her authority. She made the rules, defined the parameters, and punished with silence or shunning those who disobeyed. There was some impulse among those of us in her circle to try to move closer to the center. When you were there, you felt held and honored and privileged. When you weren't, you felt disowned, homeless, and afraid. She promised redemption and homecoming and unity if you believed as she believed and followed her path. If not, she sent you away or, worse, allowed you on the fringes of the group, where your separation shone for all to see.

I wasn't expelled from this pretend paradise, nor did I leave in any grand way. I simply turned my eyes toward other things and let it slip away. Looking back, I know that I moved away because I took a step toward greater self-honesty, and I can say that my work with her and her ideas helped me find that. I had walked that path a ways and understood it was not my path—that I needed both a firmer foundation and more freedom of thought; that, for better or worse, I had my own ideas and I wanted, hoped to find a place they were welcome. It couldn't be there. I could be true to the guru or true to myself, but not both. I chose to serve my own salvation rather than to serve that particular path.

It left me lost again, but free to search, and a bit better equipped for searching. I understood myself better, and I had learned more about life. I had reached into the realm of mystery, and it left me a little more disillusioned and a little more receptive. I didn't believe most of what the guru taught, but I had opened myself to an experience that left me in wonder, and wonder inevitably opens a door that for me had been closed. I would never again go back to being a person who needed proof, who met faith with doubt, who questioned mystery and demanded it explain itself. The path had changed me, but could not claim me to its service because, in the end, it was not a true path of healing. True paths don't claim: they allow.

Therapy has been a true path for me, and there have been others. I find help and growth in many places, some formal, some informal, some organized, some spontaneous and surprising. Every now and again, I am seduced by the charms of an easy answer, but I have learned to take what's good and leave the rest and return to what I know I can trust—honesty, accountability, love, patience, the courage to travel forward, and the people and ideas that support my healing and my growth.

There are many paths to self-discovery, to healing our self-abandonment and growing ourselves into who we can be. Some good paths are professedly religious or spiritual; others are secular and aim at practicality and a moral order without attachment to transcendence. We can enter the path with intention or look around and find ourselves there, wondering when and how we decided to travel this way.

Most of us find our way to a true path that works for us. I believe this because of what I see: people seem to find their way. Life itself is our best teacher, and the lessons are all there to be learned. The conscious choice to enter the path, whether through therapy, individual effort, or in company of like-minded travelers, lifts the heart and softens the struggles. That decision can be made anytime and as many times as needed. Go gently, go slowly, go patiently, but go. You are the treasure at the end of the never-ending path, and you are waiting to be discovered.

Wholeness does not mean perfection: it means embracing brokenness as an integral part of life. Knowing this gives me hope that human wholeness—mine, yours, ours—need not be a utopian dream, if we can use devastation as a seedbed for new life.

—Parker Palmer, American author and educator

EPIGRAPH

Wherever you go, go with all your heart.

-Confucius, Chinese philospher, circa 500BC

A Grace Note

APPENDIX A

QUICK FIXES

Offered with no apology and completely without irony, these are quick fixes to get you through the day or the moment or the hour. None of them will fix your life. That's another matter altogether, but these small things can change your mood, balance your mind, and carry you across.

- Keep a journal. Write five to ten minutes each day.
- Make gratitude lists. Even five minutes a day of searching your heart and mind for things you are grateful for will improve your happiness, your productivity, and your relationships—even if you fail to find one thing to go on the list. Imagine what happens as your list gets longer and longer.
- Walk.
- Spend time outside.
- Laugh out loud.
- Make art—music, painting, sculpture, writing, dance, drawing, crafts, sand castles.
- Dance.
- Hug.
- Smile. Just smile.
- Do something nice for someone else.

- Wear your favorite outfit.
- Put flowers in your home.
- Pamper yourself—manicure, pedicure, new hairdo, massage, facial, steam bath, whatever feels delicious.
- Take a deep breath.
- Watch a sunset.
- Watch a child.
- Have a pet.
- Check one thing off your to-do list.
- Call a friend.
- Pray.
- If you are walking fast, walk slower. If you are walking slowly, pick up the pace.
- Stand up straight.
- Make your own list of five actions you know will give you a boost or help you feel calm.

APPENDIX B

GUIDEPOSTS

These lists of words and phrases describe the elements that facilitate the path of wholeness and a few that inhibit or block it. The lists might be helpful if you feel stuck and need a prompt for how to get back on track. Or you could use them as a test to evaluate a current experience or relationship that promises help, but leaves you feeling unsure.

On the other hand, please remember that you are always the expert on you, so trust your instincts and then confirm them with a valued ally.

Self

Qualities to develop and cherish in yourself

- Curiosity
- Willingness
- Courage
- Honesty
- Openness
- Truth telling
- Focus
- Vulnerability
- Imagination
- Self-expression
- Persistence
- Humor
- Practice

Others

Qualities and features to look for in your helpers, whether they are professional helpers or friends and volunteers

- Listening
- Curiosity
- Hope
- Patience
- Warmth
- Acceptance
- Trustworthiness
- Respect
- Owning limits

- Self-awareness
- Focus
- Love
- Perception of the possible
- Universality
- Information
- Vulnerability
- Modeling positive behavior
- Healthy boundaries

Time, Place, and Context

External factors that can support you on your journey. Of course, this is individual and personal, but everyone can benefit from taking time to provide just the right atmosphere for growth and healing.

- Beauty
- Quiet
- Privacy
- Sounds, sights, and smells of nature
- Soft surfaces
- Pleasing sounds
- Cozy spots and open vistas
- Books, paper, pens, paints, pencils, scraps of fabric, art supplies
- Time: things to do and time to do nothing, regular time for meditation and for talking
- Someone to walk with
- Attention to body and mind
- Something to learn, something to teach
- Circles and squares—all shapes and sizes
- Rituals

Good Therapy

Should you decide that therapy is the right choice for you, here are some guideposts to what makes good therapy. You may notice, there isn't a single technique on the list. Techniques can be helpful, but only in the context of a positive relationship and only in reducing specific symptoms.

- Boundaries
- Ethics
- No emotional agenda for therapist
- Questions
- Listening—active
- Interest
- Respect: person, privacy, integrity, autonomy
- Warmth
- Hope (the power of possibility)
- Tolerance for feelings
- Suggestions (never answers)
- Information/education
- Confidence
- Patience
- Unconditional positive regard
- Confronting destructive patterns
- Why?
- Love
- Supportive
- Collaborative

Bad Therapy

As is the case with love, things done in the name of help that are in fact not helpful cause harm. Often in the case of the therapist, it is unintentional, but it is harm nonetheless. If you feel that any of these factors are present in a therapy relationship, talk to the therapist about it. It could be the most therapeutic thing you ever do, and that conversation will likely tell you whether this therapist is a good choice for you. If not, move on, but don't give up.

- Having all the answers—"I know more about my clients than they know about themselves."
- Quick fixes
- Labeling
- Boredom
- Judgment
- Intolerance
- Rigidity
- Lack of boundaries
- Technique over person
- Globalizing
- Indifference
- Despair
- Unconsciousness—lack of self-awareness
- Exploitation—physical or emotional—using client for own gains

APPENDIX C

HOBBY POSSIBILITIES

Here's a tiny segment of a list of possible hobbies to stimulate your imagination.

- Acting
- Archery
- Astronomy
- Backpacking
- Baseball
- Baton twirling
- Beekeeping
- Bird-watching
- Board games
- Bodybuilding
- Candle-making
- Card games
- Collecting
- Computer programming
- Cooking
- Cosplaying
- Couponing
- Creative writing
- Crochet
- Cycling
- Dance
- Digital arts
- DIY
- Dowsing
- Drawing
- Embroidery
- Fishing
- Flower arranging
- Flying
- Fossil hunting
- Gaming
- Gardening
- Genealogy
- Ghost hunting
- Glassblowing
- Gunsmithing

- Ice skating
- Jewelry-making
- Jigsaw puzzles
- Juggling
- Kayaking
- Knife-making
- Knitting
- Lace-making
- Lapidary
- Legos
- Lock-picking (Found on several lists of hobbies— no kidding)
- Macrame
- Magic
- Martial arts
- Motorsports
- Mountain climbing
- Music
- Orienteering
- Origami
- Pets
- Photography
- Pottery
- Puzzles
- Quilting
- Sailing
- Scuba
- Shopping
- Singing
- Snowboarding
- Whittling
- Yoga

The list could go on and on. The only requirements are that you find activities that give you something to do, something to love, and something to hope for. Try new things or add something to your current hobby. Take a lesson, join a new group, find a new partner. If it doesn't fit, let it go. If it is interesting but not yet compelling, stay with it for a bit and see what happens. If you love it, if it feels like home, then you know that it's right for you, that it will lead you farther down your true path.

APPENDIX D

THE TEN BEST BOOKS ON PSYCHOTHERAPY EVER

In alphabetical order because I keep changing the rankings. There are actually eleven on the list because I remembered another. Despite this evolution, these titles remain relevant and important over time.

Adler, Alfred. (1924). *The Practice and Theory of Individual Psychology*. New York: Harcourt Brace.

Brown, L. S. (2004). *Subversive Dialogues: Theory in Feminist Therapy*. New York: Basic Books.

Frankl, Viktor. (1963). *Man's Search for Meaning: An Introduction to Logotherapy*. Boston: Beacon Press.

Howard, Stephen. (2008). *The Heart and Soul of the Therapist: Rage, Fear, Desire, Loss, and Love in the Psychotherapy Relationship*. Lanham: UPA.

Jung, C. G. (1968). *Analytical Psychology: Its Theory and Practice*. New York: Vintage Books.

Kopp, Sheldon B. (1972). *If You Meet Your Buddha on the Road, Kill Him! The Pilgrimage of Psychotherapy Patients*. Palo Alto: Science and Behavior Books.

May, Rollo. (1989). *The Art of Counseling*. New York: Gardner Press.

Miller, Alice. (1996). *The Drama of the Gifted Child: The Search for the True Self*. New York: Basic Books.

Moore, Thomas. (1992). *Care of the Soul.* New York: HarperCollins.

Rogers, Carl, & Kramer, Peter. (1995). *On Becoming a Person: A Therapist's View of Psychotherapy.* Mariner.

Yalom, Irvin. (2012). *Love's Executioner and Other Tales of Psychotherapy.* New York: Basic Books.

APPENDIX E

RESOURCES

Books and other places to find inspiration. Each of these has provided some guidance for my path. Some of them may guide you as well. Follow your intuition. Trust your instincts. But never stop learning.

Angelou, M. (1969). *I Know Why the Caged Bird Sings.* New York: Random House.

Angelou, M. (1990). *I Shall Not Be Moved.* New York: Bantam Books.

Everything Angelou has ever written.

Arendt, H. (1958). T *he Human Condition.* Chicago: University of Chicago Press.

Bateson, G. (1972). *Steps to an Ecology of Mind.* New York: Chandler.

Bennett, W. J. (1996). *The Book of Virtues.* New York: Simon & Schuster.

Bolen, J. (1984). *Goddesses in Everywoman: A New Psychology of Women.* New York: Harper & Row.

Bolen, J. (1989). *Gods in Everyman: A New Psychology of Men's Lives and Loves.* New York: Harper and Row.

Bolen, J. (2001). *Goddesses in Older Women: Archetypes in Women over Fifty.* New York: HarperCollins.

Bolz-Weber, N. (2013). *Pastrix: The Cranky, Beautiful Faith of a Sinner & Saint.* New York: Jericho Books.

Borysenko, J. (1990). *Guilt Is the Teacher, Love Is the Lesson.* New York: Warner Books.

Borysenko, J. (1993). *Fire in the Soul: A New Psychology of Spiritual Optimism.* New York: Warner.

Bragg, R. (1999). *All Over But the Shoutin'.* New York: Random House.

Brooks, D. (2015). *The Road to Character.* New York: Random House.

Brown, B. (2010). *The Gifts of Imperfection.* Center City, MN: Hazelden.

Bulfinch. T. (1993). *Bulfinch's Mythology.* New York: The Modern Library.

Campbell, J. (1972). *Myths We Live By.* New York: Bantam. Also: *The Hero with a Thousand Faces; The Masks of God; The Power of Myth.*

Chessler, P. (1972). *Women and Madness.* New York: Avon.

Coelho, P. (1988). *The Alchemist.* New York: Harper Perennial.

Csikszentmihalyi, M. (1990). *Flow: The Psychology of Optimal Experience.* New York: Harper & Row.

DeMello, A. (1988). *Taking Flight.* New York: Image Books. Also try *The Way to Love* or *Song of the Bird.*

Dinnerstein, D. (1976). *The Mermaid and the Minotaur: Sexual Arrangements and Human Malaise.* New York: Harper & Row.

Duhigg, C. (2012). *The Power of Habit: Why We Do What We Do in Life and Business.* New York: Random House.

Edinger, E. F. (1972). *Ego and Archetype.* New York: Putnam's/Jung Foundation.

Estes, C. P. (1992). *Women Who Run with the Wolves: Myths and Stories of the Wild Woman Archetype.* New York: Ballantine Books.

Freud, S. (1965). *The Psychopathology of Everyday Life.* New York: W.W. Norton. Also: many other works, most of them collected into *The Complete Psychological Works of Sigmund Freud,* 24 volumes.

Friday, N. (1977). *My Mother / My Self.* New York: Delacorte Press.

Gaiman, N. (2013). *The Ocean at the End of the Lane*. New York: William Morrow Books.

Gawande, A. (2014). *Being Mortal: Medicine and What Matters in the End*. New York: Metropolitan Books.

Gilbert, E. (2007). *Eat, Pray, Love*. New York: Penguin.

Haidt, J. (2006). *The Happiness Hypothesis: Finding Modern Truth in Ancient Wisdom*. New York: Basic Books.

Haidt, J. (2012). *The Righteous Mind*. New York: Vintage Books, a division of Random House.

Hall, J. M. (1986). *The Jungian Experience: Analysis and Individuation*. Toronto: Inner City.

Hamilton, E. (1942). *Mythology*. Boston: Little, Brown.

Hillman, J. (1996). *The Soul's Code: In Search of Character and Calling*. New York: Random House.

Horney, K. (1942). *Self-Analysis*. New York: Norton. Several other titles are worth reading: *Our Inner Conflicts*; *Feminine Psychology*; *Neurosis and Human Growth*.

Houston, J. (1987). *The Search for the Beloved: Journeys in Mythology and Sacred Psychology*. Los Angeles: Tarcher.

Jacobi. J. (1942). *The Psychology of C. G. Jung*. London: Routledge & Kegan.

Johnson, R. (1986). *Inner Work: Using Dreams and Active Imagination for Personal Growth*. San Francisco: Harper.

Johnson, R. (1989). *He: Understanding Masculine Psychology*. New York: Harper & Row.

Johnson, R. (1989). *She: Understanding Feminine Psychology*. New York: Harper & Row.

Johnson, R. (1990). *Femininity Lost and Regained*. New York: Harper & Row.

Johnson, R. (1991). *Owning Your Own Shadow*. San Francisco: Harper.

Johnson, R., with Ruhl, J. (1998). *Balancing Heaven and Earth: A Memoir of Visions, Dreams, and Realizations*. San Francisco: Harper.

Jones, Alan. 1985. *Soulmaking: The Desert Way of Spirituality*. San Francisco: Harper.

Jung, C. G. (1933). *Modern Man in Search of a Soul*. San Diego: Harcourt Brace.

Jung, C. G. (1963). *Memories, Dreams and Reflections*. (A. Jaffe, Ed.), (R. Winston & C. Winston, trans.) New York: Pantheon.

Jung, C., & Kerenya, C. (1949). *Essays on a Science of Mythology*. Princeton: Princeton University Press.

Jung, C. G., von Franz, M. L., Henderson, J. L., Jacobi, J., & Jaffe, A. (1964). *Man and His Symbols*. New York: Doubleday.

Karr, M. (2005). *The Liars' Club*. New York: Penguin.

Keen, S., & Fox, A. V. (1989). *Your Mythic Journey*. New York: Tarcher.

Kerr, J. (1993). *A Most Dangerous Method: The Story of Jung, Freud, and Sabina Spielrein*. New York: Knopf.

Keyes, K. (1972). *Handbook to Higher Consciousness*. New York: Love Line Books, 5th edition.

Kubler-Ross, E. (1969). *On Death and Dying*. New York: Simon & Schuster/Touchstone.

Kushner, H. (2002). *Living a Life That Matters*. New York: Anchor. Also, *When Bad Things Happen to Good People*.

Lakoff, G., & Johnson, M. (1980). *Metaphors We Live By*. Chicago: University of Chicago Press.

Lamott, A. (1999). *Traveling Mercies: Some Thoughts on Faith*. New York: Anchor.

Lamott, A. (2014). *Small Victories: Spotting Improbable Moments of Grace*. New York: Riverhead Books.

LeGuin, Ursula K. (1989). *Dancing at the Edge of the World: Thoughts on Words, Women, Places*. New York: Grove Press.

Leonard, L. (1982). *The Wounded Woman: Healing the Father-Daughter Relationship*. Boston: Shambala.

Leonard, L. (1984). *On the Way to the Wedding: Transforming the Love Relationship*. Boston: Shambala.

Leonard, L. (1990). *Witness to the Fire: Creativity and the Veil of Addiction.* Boston: Shambala

Leonard, L. (1993). *Meeting the Madwoman: An Inner Challenge for Feminine Spirit.* New York: Bantam.

Lewis, C. S. (1943). *Mere Christianity.* New York: MacMillan. Also: *The Problem of Pain; The Lion, The Witch and the Wardrobe; The Four Loves; Till We Have Faces*; and many others.

Lopez, B. (1990). *Crow and Weasel.* New York: North Point Press.

Luke, H. M. (1985). *The Way of Woman: Awakening the Perennial Feminine.* New York: Doubleday.

Luke, H. M. (1987). *Old Age: Journey into Simplicity.* New York: Parabola.

May, R. (1991). *The Cry for Myth.* New York: W. W. Norton. Also: *Love and Will; The Meaning of Anxiety; Man's Search for Himself; The Courage to Create*; and others.

Merton, T. (1948). *The Seven Storey Mountain.* New York: Harcourt Brace.

Miller, A. (1981). *The Drama of the Gifted Child: The Search for the True Self.* New York: Basic Books.

Miller, W. R., & C'de Baca, J. (2001). *Quantum Change.* New York: Guilford Press.

Mlodinow, L. (2013). *Subliminal: How Your Unconscious Mind Rules Your Behavior.* New York: Vintage.

Moore, T. (1992). *Care of the Soul: A Guide for Cultivating Depth and Sacredness in Everyday Life.* New York: HarperCollins.

Mother Teresa. (2002). *No Greater Love.* Oakland: New World Library.

Murdock, M. (1990). *The Heroine's Journey.* Boston: Shambala.

Nussbaum, M. (2001). *Upheavals of Thought: The Intelligence of Emotions.* Cambridge: Cambridge University Press.

Pennebaker, J. W. (1997). *Opening Up: The Healing Power of Expressing Emotions.* New York: Guilford Publications.

Perez, N. (2013). *New and Selected Poems 1981–2013.* Fernandina Beach, FL: Charlie Chan Press.

Reeves, P. (1999). *Women's Intuition: Unlocking the Wisdom of the Body*. Berkeley: Conari Press.

Reeves, P. (2003). *Heart Sense: Unlocking Your Highest Purpose and Deepest Desires*. Berkeley: Conari Press.

Remen, R. (1996). *Kitchen Table Wisdom: Stories that Heal*. New York: Riverhead Books.

Rich, A. (1976). *Of Woman Born: Motherhood as Experience and Institution*. New York: W. W. Norton.

Rogers, C. (1961). *On Becoming a Person: A Therapist's View of Psychotherapy*. London: Constable.

Roosevelt, E. (2011). *You Learn by Living: Eleven Keys for a More Fulfilling Life*. New York: Harper Perennial, 50th Anv. Edition.

Ruiz, M. (1997). *The Four Agreements*. San Rafael, CA: Amber-Allen Publishing.

Sacks, O. (1998). *The Man Who Mistook His Wife for a Hat and Other Clinical Tales*. New York: Touchstone.

Sacks, O. (2015). *Gratitude*. New York: Alfred A. Knopf.

Saint Therese of Lisieux. (1996). *Story of a Soul: The Autobiography of Saint Therese of Lisieux*. Translated by John Clarke, O.C.D. Washington: ICS Publications.

Stein, M., Ed. (1995). *Jungian Analysis*. (2nd Ed.) Chicago: Open Court.

Theroux, P. (2012). *The Tao of Travel: Enlightenments from Lives on the Road*. New York: Mariner Books.

Tillich, P. (1952). *The Courage to Be*. New York: Yale University Press.

VonFranz, J. L. (1980). *Alchemy: An Introduction to the Symbolism and the Psychology*. Toronto: Inner City.

Walker, B. G. (1985). *The Crone: Woman of Age, Wisdom, and Power*. San Francisco: Harper San Francisco.

Walker, B. G. (1990). *Women's Rituals*. San Francisco: Harper San Francisco.

Whitmont, E. C. (1973). *The Symbolic Quest*. New York: Harper & Row.

Woodman, M. (1982). *Addiction to Perfection: The Still Unravished Bride*. Toronto: Inner City.

Woodman, M. (1985). *The Pregnant Virgin: The Process of Psychological Transformation*. Toronto: Inner City.

Woodman, M. (1990). *The Ravaged Bridegroom: Masculinity in Women*. Toronto: Inner City.

Woodman, M. (2000). *Bone: Dying into Life*. New York: Viking.

Also: Everything by Woodman is worth reading. She has a number of wonderful audio and video recordings as well as books not mentioned here.

Whyte, D. (2015). *Consolations: The Solace, Nourishment and Underlying Meaning of Everyday Words*. Many Rivers Press.

ACKNOWLEDGMENTS

Here's something I've learned. I never really know what's going to happen next. Most of the things I worry about never happen and life is seldom exactly what I expected it would be. I've had my share of disappointments, but these are far outweighed by the gifts I've been given.

I am grateful to so many people.

From the beginning, I was among those fortunate to have people in my life who loved me and who were trying the best they knew how to lead good lives and add good things to the world and could model that for me. I grew up in a town that, despite a normal share of the world's problems, was populated mostly by decent folks living decent lives, like most towns, I think.

At school, I learned from dedicated teachers, each in his or her own way, an example of a life of purpose and the value of learning. At work, in each of my careers, I met and shared challenges and pleasures with a diverse collection of people who each helped me learn and grow. I've had teachers and mentors and adversaries and friends and they've all added vital bits to my education.

When I began to think about extending my love of writing into the wider world by publishing, I knew virtually nothing about that world. So I began to read and study and research and ask questions and talk to people who did know. I heard a lot of negative things about how hard it is to get published and how cutthroat the industry could be and how few authors made money with their books and how I should just give up the idea. I can't say why I didn't, but I can say that I'm glad I didn't. It's been great fun so far.

Oh, some of what I heard is true enough. It is hard—to write, to get published, to sell books, all of it. Worthwhile ventures are seldom easy. And, yet, I have so much to be grateful for. I've met so many warm-hearted, kind, generous people in the book business, also funny, interesting, talented, quirky people who have energized my life in unexpected ways.

So here you go, in no particular order, thank you: Patricia, Nancy, Nola, Emily, Don, Andrea, Sue, Beth, Cathy, Kathleen, Sonia, Carolyn, Cheri, Win, Terri, David, Rick, Tom, Jane, Sandy, and Karen. Thanks for sharing your lessons and experience and adding color to my days. I'm grateful also for those I've met as the result of moving around in the world as an author, the people at The Book Loft in Fernandina Beach, Florida, who have been the most generous of hosts, and the people who have attended book signings and talks and some of whom have become treasured friends.

Particular thanks go to Patricia Charpentier for being my guide to the publishing business and for doing such extraordinarily good work for me on all my projects.

Thank you to Cheri Madison for amazingly efficient and effective editing. Having a good editor is a little like having a good surgeon—they may cause you some pain along the way, but they save your life! Thanks to Andrea Patten and Nancy Blanton for peer support and professional guidance that has kept me on track and excited about what we do.

Several people give their time and energy to this project by reading and commenting on my stories before I called it done and sent it off to the publisher. My sincerest gratitude goes to Linda Lanzarotta, Joan Daniel, Harold Haddle, Marsha Joiner, Mary Ellen Hughes, Tom Hughes, and Beth McKibben-Nee. Any problems that remain are entirely my own responsibility, but, thanks to these folks, I was saved from myself a few times.

My deepest gratitude goes to everyone who read *Traveling Stories*. Of course, I loved it when you said you liked it or, even more, when you said you connected with something in it in a personal way. Thank you for that. But I'm also grateful to anyone who took the time to read it even if I never heard from you at all. You gave the gift of your time and I know how valuable that is.

Julie and Jennifer, you hold my heart in your hands. I love you.

Mark, you make my sun come up and give me more of love and laughter and joy each day than I expected to get in a lifetime.

You see, I really don't know what is going to happen next, but so far; it's been very, very good.

ABOUT THE AUTHOR

Terri Clements Dean, PhD, is a clinical psychologist in private practice and author of *Traveling Stories: Lessons from the Journey of Life* and its companion journal, *Traveling Stories Journal.* A former anthropologist, she has also studied philosophy, belief systems, gender knowledge, and psychology with a focus on symbolic systems. She has diverse administrative and clinical experience in private and  public mental health settings as well as private practice. Her broad interests and extensive mental health background give her a unique perspective in understanding each person's life, as well as a deep well of resources to guide her work as a clinician, lecturer, and writer.

She believes that wholeness is our birthright and that life is a journey toward claiming our deepest, best selves. Find more about what she's learned on her journey at www.terridean.us.

Terri lives on a magical island in northeast Florida with her husband, Mark, and their best canine buddy, Sunny.

Terri would love to hear from you. Go to www.terridean.us and send her your comments or stories of traveling the path of wholeness.

Traveling Stories Reviews

"This book is a celebration of the complex elegance of our *human beingness*. Our stories are the fiber that knit together cultures, communities, families, and friendships; Dr. Dean offers us a treasure box of storied wisdom and remembrance. A rich must read."

— Paula M. Reeves, PhD, mythographer, psychotherapist,
and author of *Women's Intuition: Unlocking the Wisdom of the Body* and
Heart Sense: Unlocking Your Highest Purpose and Deepest Desires

"There are so many beautiful parts to Dr. Dean's writing, things to hold onto during the dark hours that just might be enough to see you through."

— Jennifer Angier, CEO, Black Bear Lodge,
Foundations Recovery Network

"*Traveling Stories: Lessons from the Journey of Life* is a captivating, enlightening yet extremely entertaining book. Terri Dean has a true gift to interpret meaning from everyday occurrences. Unabashedly, she allows us entrance into her life and, without hesitation, shares personal revelations on how to enjoy the process of revising and reworking our own life stories. An engrossing must read that provides valuable insight into how life is a teacher if we will simply learn to listen."

— Terri Wright, author, lecturer

"Thank you for writing this book and sharing the stories with the world. I thoroughly enjoyed reading it cover to cover and look forward to the sequel."

— Virginia Dunlap, artist and poet

"I just returned from a cruise through the Bahamas. It was fun. I just wanted to let you know that the best part of my trip was the time I spent alone, on the quiet part of the ship, under the sun, in the breeze, reading your book! It was a great read. I look forward to seeking and reading more of your work! Thank you!"

— Kelly, investment banker

"Dr. Teresa Dean is a gifted storyteller and author. To read *Traveling Stories* is not only to travel along in one's mind's eye with Dr. Dean but also to experience the courage, love, and forgiveness of each of the individuals she meets in her travels. A must read, a personal growth experience for me, and I can't wait to read her next book.

— Molly McCue, licensed professional counselor

"You have written a wonderful book. You have managed to distill insights from your specific life experiences and transform them into universal truths. I had no idea what to do with my dreams until I read your book. I am enjoying that new consciousness and what I might learn. I also love the way you structured the book's chapters with such meaningful quotes. I can only imagine how challenging that must have been. They are perfectly placed and set the tone for the chapters that follow. I think your book should receive wide attention and a huge audience. I think I need to buy multiple copies for my friends and sisters. You have written an exceptional book and I hope there will be more to follow."

— Mary, reader

"From the moment I began reading *Traveling Stories: Lessons from the Journey of Life*, I was hooked. I'm on the second read and continue to highlight passages that speak to my heart. [This book] will gently guide me and thousands of other readers as we take that next step into our own journey of life. We all have lessons to be learned. Life talks to us. Listen."

— Barbara Ryan, *St. Mary's Magazine*

"It may seem odd to say, but I found *Traveling Stories* to be very comforting. I enjoyed the humor, and I learned some things too, but in the end, I mainly felt comforted by it. I love that! Thank you for writing it."

— Sara, reader

"I bought this book because I was intrigued by the idea of the four questions and hoped to find some answers. While I still have questions, I have bought more copies of the book for 30 of my friends and relatives, so I'd say I liked it a lot. It's thought provoking and enjoyable to read. Highly recommend."

— Ben, business owner

"What I liked best is that you can read for a few minutes each night and still get something to take with you and use in your everyday life."

— Claudette, dancer, mother

"This book is a collection of charming and thoughtful stories. Dr. Dean does a great job of weaving the stories with myths, tales, and anecdotes to show you how small, everyday things can change your view of yourself and your life, as well as how big revelations can happen anytime in your life. It is well written and easy to read. Dr. Dean had studied anthropology and psychology, and if you pay attention, you can learn a lot when reading this book about embracing what life throws at you. The author uses quotes of other people at the beginning of each chapter, and some of them are brilliant! I recommend it!"

— Amazon review

"Dr. Dean's book is a very interesting read. It is well written, warm, and very thoughtful. The stories she tells make one think of their own experiences and how they relate to themselves. It imparts a softness and kindness in the stories that are truly thought provoking. I think it will make you ponder your own life and actions and those around you. I am very happy I bought it. I will pass it to my daughter shortly. Good lessons learned."

— Amazon review

"This book is a creative story of stories from the lives of real people and what happened to them. The collection is refreshing in that most all worked out well and that's how I personally like endings to be. It brings to mind a clear example [of] why we should believe that everything happens for a reason, and we don't have to get depressed over depressing things happening in our lives for we don't know at the time that it is all going to turn out for our good somehow. When we feel scared, overwhelmed, and vulnerable, the stories in this book make everything ok."

— Amazon review

Also available from Terri Clements Dean and LifeStory Publishing

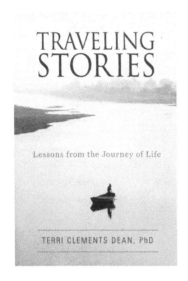

Traveling Stories:
Lessons from the Journey of Life
by Terri Clements Dean

Stories to help you heal, grow, and flourish

There Are Really Only Four Questions:

Who am I?
Where to I belong?
What matters?
How do I live my life?

These *Traveling Stories*, drawn from Dr. Terri Clements Dean's journeys, her psychology practice, and her life, focus on the ways in which life's lessons make their way to us in the small things, in the unexpected, in the struggles, and in the ordinary, gently guiding us to discover the next step in his or her unique journey. Together they assure that the lessons are there to be learned; all we have to do is be impeccably honest with ourselves, pay careful attention, work hard at what we learn, and trust the process.

Also, the companion book by Terri Clements Dean, *Traveling Stories Journal: A Guide to Discovering Your Own Life Lessons*

A personal workbook to help you heal, grow, and flourish

The cure for what ails you starts with telling your story. Each human life is an extraordinary story made up of many small stories, moments, and themes that together shape the journey and the traveler. *Traveling Stories Journal: A Guide to Discovering Your Own Life Lessons*, companion book to *Traveling Stories: Lessons from the Journey of Life*, is designed to help you tell your story and, in so doing, make your next best life.

CPSIA information can be obtained
at www.ICGtesting.com
Printed in the USA
LVHW01s1006160917

548787LV00003B/3/P